Teach Yourself VISUALLY™

Bass Guitar

Hear Audio Tracks from This Book at wiley.com!

In case you need a little help in understanding how a particular piece is supposed to sound, we've included audio tracks from this book on our Web site. You can access those files via this link: www.wiley.com/go/tyvbassguitar.

Here's a list of the tracks that you'll find there:

Teach Yourself VISUALLY™

Bass Guitar

Visual®

by Ryan Williams and Richard Hammond

BICENTENNIAL
1807
WILEY
2007
BICENTENNIAL

Wiley Publishing, Inc.

For general information on our other products and services or to obtain technical support please contact our Customer Care Department within the U.S. at (800) 762-2974, outside the U.S. at (317) 572-3993 or fax (317) 572-4002.

Wiley also publishes its books in a variety of electronic formats. Some content that appears in print may not be available in electronic books. For more information about Wiley products, please visit our web site at www.wiley.com.

Library of Congress Control Number: 2006926290

ISBN-13: 978-0-470-04850-4
ISBN-10: 0-470-04850-6

Printed in the United States of America

10 9 8 7 6 5 4 3 2 1

Book production by Wiley Publishing, Inc. Composition Services

Praise for the Teach Yourself VISUALLY Series

I just had to let you and your company know how great I think your books are. I just purchased my third Visual book (my first two are dog-eared now!) and, once again, your product has surpassed my expectations. The expertise, thought, and effort that go into each book are obvious, and I sincerely appreciate your efforts. Keep up the wonderful work!

—Tracey Moore (Memphis, TN)

I have several books from the Visual series and have always found them to be valuable resources.

—Stephen P. Miller (Ballston Spa, NY)

Thank you for the wonderful books you produce. It wasn't until I was an adult that I discovered how I learn—visually. Although a few publishers out there claim to present the material visually, nothing compares to Visual books. I love the simple layout. Everything is easy to follow. And I understand the material! You really know the way I think and learn. Thanks so much!

—Stacey Han (Avondale, AZ)

Like a lot of other people, I understand things best when I see them visually. Your books really make learning easy and life more fun.

—John T. Frey (Cadillac, MI)

I am an avid fan of your Visual books. If I need to learn anything, I just buy one of your books and learn the topic in no time. Wonders! I have even trained my friends to give me Visual books as gifts.

—Illona Bergstrom (Aventura, FL)

I write to extend my thanks and appreciation for your books. They are clear, easy to follow, and straight to the point. Keep up the good work! I bought several of your books and they are just right! No regrets! I will always buy your books because they are the best.

—Seward Kollie (Dakar, Senegal)

Credits

Acquisitions Editor
Pam Mourouzis

Project Editor
Suzanne Snyder

Copy Editor
Lori Cates Hand

Technical Editor
Scott Maxwell

Editorial Manager
Christina Stambaugh

Publisher
Cindy Kitchel

Vice President and Executive Publisher
Kathy Nebenhaus

Interior Design
Kathie Rickard
Elizabeth Brooks

Cover Design
José Almaguer

Interior Photography
Matt Bowen

Photographic Assistant
Andrew Hanson

Special Thanks...

To Reno's Music (www.guitarhotline.com), especially Steve Rohrer, owner, for granting us permission to show photographs of its equipment.

About the Authors

Ryan Williams is a bassist based in Indianapolis, Indiana. He's shared the stage and studio with everybody and everything from Grammy-award-winning hip-hop artists to a full band of bagpipes and drums. He received his master's degree in music technology from the Indiana University School of Music in 2003. He's the author of *Windows XP Digital Music For Dummies,* and has written several articles and tutorials on music and music technology for several publications and websites. He's a frequent panelist on digital music and home studios at music conferences around the nation.

Technical editor **Richard Hammond**, originally from New Zealand, is now based in New York City. He started playing electric bass at age 13, and by age 20 he was one of the most in-demand acoustic and electric bassists in Auckland, playing numerous studio, touring, and television dates. He moved to Boston's Berklee College of Music in 1991, earning a bachelor's degree in performance, after which followed a master's degree in jazz from the Manhattan School of Music in 1996. Richard quickly established himself as a musician able to move freely between a vast array of styles with equal depth, fluidity, and sense of groove. As a professional bassist, he has recorded and toured with a diverse array of bands and solo artists, including Jonatha Brooke, Chiara Civello, the East Village Opera Company, Erasure, House of Red, Anjelique Kidjo, and Dar Williams.

Acknowledgments

This book could not have been completed without the tireless efforts of my acquisitions editor Pam Mourouzis, project editor Suzanne Snyder, copy editor Lori Cates Hand, and technical editors Richard Hammond and Scott Maxwell. Thanks are also due to Steve Hayes, Matt Fecher, and everybody at Indianapolismusic.net, About Music in Broad Ripple, and the Indiana University School of Music.

I owe a great debt of gratitude to bassist and model extraordinaire Sharon Koltick. Please contact her at http://sharonjk.com, hire her, and pay her well.

Thanks to the bassists who have inspired my playing over the years: Doug Pinnick, Meshell Ndegeocello, Doug Wimbish, Bootsy Collins, Seth Horan, and James Jamerson.

Finally, many thanks to my wife, Jennifer Hughes, for putting up with the odd writing schedules, the low rumbling noises emanating from my practice room, the impulse purchases of vintage bass gear, and her love and patience in general.

Table of Contents

chapter 1 An Introduction to Bass Guitar

chapter 2 Parts of Your Bass Guitar

chapter 3 Holding Your Bass Guitar

chapter 4 Tuning Your Bass Guitar

chapter 5 — Basic Fretboard Fingering

chapter 6 — Plucking and Picking

chapter 7 Play Your First Scales

chapter 8 Playing with Chords

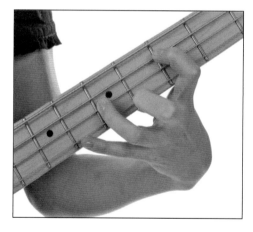

chapter 9 · Common Chord Progressions

chapter 10 · Basic Rhythms

chapter 11   Slapping and Popping

chapter 12   Getting Your Tone

chapter 13 **Buying a Bass Guitar and Amplifier**

chapter 14 **Care for Your Gear**

chapter 15 — Some Last Words

chapter 1

An Introduction to Bass Guitar

This is where you learn what the bass guitar is and what it does. More importantly, though, this is hopefully the beginning of many good times playing and enjoying music. Let's get started!

What the Bass Guitar Does

Most of the popular music you hear today is built on the foundation of the bass guitar. It provides the basic building blocks necessary to make a song, and it can also add just the right part here or there to make some timeless music.

Elements of Bass Guitar Playing

Whether you listen to pop, rock, jazz, folk, funk, or most other genres of music, chances are you've heard a bass guitar in the mix somewhere. Since it was created and popularized in the 1950s by Leo Fender, the bass guitar has become an indispensable part of the music of today. Far from just being a rhythm-section instrument, bassists from Sting to Bootsy Collins to Victor Wooten have moved from the background of the rhythm section to the forefront of popular music and made sure that the bass guitar claims a central role in many bands. When you become a good bassist, there will always be a group waiting for you.

A good bass guitarist combines rhythm, harmony, and style into a package that makes a song sing and a body want to dance. Let's take a look at each of those elements.

Rhythm

The first duty of the bass guitar is to keep the rhythm. Keeping the pulse of a song is central to your role as a bassist. Whether it's a simple country two-step or a complicated jazz-fusion riff, the bass guitar always makes sure the rhythm and tempo are clearly defined.

Most times, you'll be playing along with the kick drum of a drum set; however, you could also be working together with the player of a different rhythm instrument or just holding the rhythm all by yourself. In any of these cases, it's vital that you keep the rhythm and tempo of the song moving and clearly defined. Check out Chapter 10 for more information on common rhythms.

Everybody has rhythm. It's in the way that you walk or the way that you talk. All you're doing here is translating your natural rhythm to the bass guitar. Relax and let it come to you as you practice.

CONTINUED ON NEXT PAGE

Harmony

At the same time the bass guitar is keeping the rhythm, it's also providing the basic harmony for the song. In most cases, the bass note defines the key of the song and the chord the instruments are playing at any time in the song. Where the bass leads, the others follow.

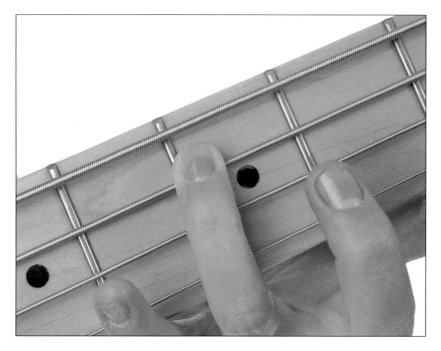

The notes you choose to play create the character of the song, so it's important to learn as much as you can about what makes a chord sound the way it does, and how to make your bass lines flow easily from one chord to the next. This contributes greatly to making the song memorable and worth listening to. Look at chapters 8 and 9 for more information on chords and harmony.

Remember, all songs are made up of melodies over a bed of rhythm and harmony. Other instruments build on what you create and define.

Style

When you can keep a rhythm and know the song's harmony, all that's left is to play the song with style. Style is a word that's hard to define sometimes, but you always know when you hear it. You might hear it called "swinging," "rocking," or "grooving," but it always means that the bass guitar part is exactly where it should be: playing its role and making sure everything goes smoothly.

Style might be the hardest part of the bass guitar to master, but the road to style is based on being comfortable and having fun. The more you practice with your bass guitar and the more you listen to the bass guitar's role in music, the more comfortable you'll be playing it. The more comfortable you are, the more fun you'll have. When you're comfortable and having fun, the style will naturally come to you.

Get Started

It's possible for you to play your first song the same day you get your first bass guitar and amplifier. With just a little time and effort, you can be on your way.

Some Basics

YOUR BASS GUITAR

You don't need to buy an expensive instrument to start. A good-quality starter model will help both your playing and your budget. Chapter 13 tells you what to look for when you're buying your first bass guitar.

YOUR AMPLIFIER

Again, you don't need an expensive, six-foot-tall mountain of speakers and circuits to get started. A small practice amplifier enables you to hear your bass without irritating your family or your neighbors. Chapter 13 also helps you with choosing the right amp.

THE ELEMENTS OF PLAYING A NOTE

Although it might take some time to fully master the tricks and intricacies of the bass guitar, the fundamental parts—*fretting* a note and *plucking* it—are something you do the very first day. Add a couple more notes in the right rhythm, and you've got a basic song ready to go.

Chapter 5 shows you more about fretting a note, whereas Chapter 6 teaches you how to pluck one. The metal strips on the bass, called *frets* (you'll read about frets in Chapter 2), help to keep your notes in tune. Get the basics of those chapters down, and you're ready to go. The rest of the chapters add to your knowledge of the bass guitar and make you a well-rounded player. It's best to start at the beginning of the book and follow the chapters in order, but you can always feel free to jump back to other chapters for reference as you build skill and experience.

Your Milestones

Playing the bass guitar means learning something new every day. The key is making sure you keep learning. And you keep learning by practicing.

Although learning the bass guitar is a journey, it doesn't have to be a race. You'll learn more by keeping a steady pace than by going in fits and starts. It's important to make time every day to play the bass guitar in a place where you have as few distractions as possible.

Make Time for Practice

You don't have to devote every waking moment of your day to learning how to play the bass guitar. In the beginning, it's important to set a regular practice time and stick to it, even if it's for only a brief time. Try setting aside 20 minutes at first every day to go over the basics of the bass guitar. Pretty soon, you can expand it to half an hour spent warming up, reviewing those basics, and learning new material. Pretty soon, you could be up to an hour or more of serious practice time. Your playing will improve with the more time you spend practicing; however, it's important at first to get into the habit of practicing. Habits are hard to break, but the creation of good habits will only help you get better.

Find the Right Place

There are a couple of good reasons why musicians are often banished to the garage or basement to practice. One, sometimes they can be a little loud. Two, and more importantly, it gives them a space where nothing is happening beyond the activity of practicing. Just as it's difficult to read Shakespeare while the radio is on and the television is blaring, it's difficult to concentrate on practicing the bass guitar with other things going on around you. Find a quiet, comfortable place to practice, and you'll see that having fewer distractions means you learn more quickly.

Notice the items in the picture. These are essential items to your practice space:

- A comfortable chair, preferably without arms
- A CD or mp3 player to listen to songs or examples
- A music stand to hold paper (or this book) for easy viewing while playing

Finally, make sure your practice space is out of the way, so that people aren't constantly coming through and distracting you. You don't have to devote an entire room to practicing; your bedroom or living room will work. Just make sure that the only thing happening in there at that designated time is you enjoying your bass guitar practice.

TIP

Practice should never be a boring chore. When you practice, play what you like, set many goals, and you'll never get enough.

chapter 2

Parts of Your Bass Guitar

Bass guitars come in many shapes and sizes, and even have varying numbers of strings. All of them have parts in common, however. This chapter introduces you to each part and shows why it is a valuable part of your new instrument. By the time you're done with this chapter, you'll have essential knowledge of how a bass guitar works.

Parts of the Bass Guitar

Each part of the bass guitar plays an essential role in how the instrument sounds and feels when it's played.

Basic Parts

Each model and style of bass guitar might have different variations on these parts, giving each instrument an individual character. The only way to understand this is to play a wide variety of instruments and pay close attention to how they sound. Visit a musical-instrument store and try out as many basses as you can to help your ear hear these differences.

Still, the basic functions of each part are common across all bass guitars. Each bass guitar includes the following parts:

- The head
- The body
- The neck
- The bridge
- Strings
- One or more pickups
- Volume, tone, and other control knobs

All bass guitars have the first six parts and a variation of the seventh part in the preceding list. Each configuration has some advantages over the others. What you play and how you sound depend on your personal preferences.

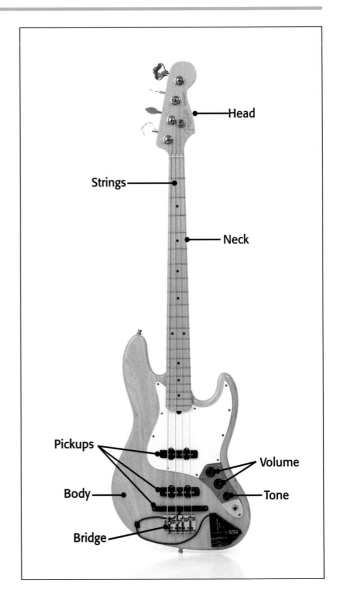

The Head

At one end of the bass guitar is the *head* (or *headstock*). The shape of the head can vary wildly from one manufacturer to another; however, they all provide one important function. The head holds the *tuning gears* of the bass, which are used to tune the strings to the correct pitch.

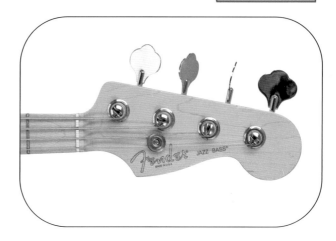

Parts of the Head

The tuning gears are turned to the left or right to raise or lower the pitch. They can appear all on one side of the head, or they can be placed on both sides of the head.

The head of the bass meets the neck at the *nut,* a piece of plastic, bone, or similar material that supports the strings, spaces them correctly, and starts the portion of the bass guitar's neck where notes are played.

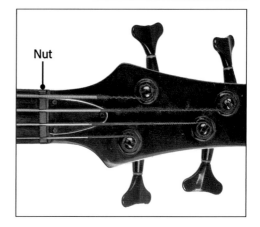

Nut

The tuning gears can be either open (where the gear itself is exposed) as in the photo or closed (where the gear is covered).

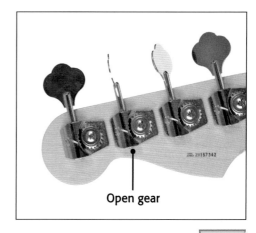

Open gear

The Body

The body accounts for the bulk of the bass guitar's weight. It also can come in many different shapes and sizes, depending on the bass guitar's manufacturer. In fact, some companies have trademark shapes that are recognizable on sight.

Body Details

COLOR AND MATERIALS

Depending on the wood used to make the body, it can make the tone sound anywhere from dark and woody to bright and snappy. It also provides the mounting surface for all of the other bass guitar parts, including the neck, bridge, and pickups.

The one part of the body that doesn't make that much difference to the bass guitar's tone is the color. There are many beautiful finishes and colors available for your instrument; however, you should use your ears first in choosing an instrument.

The type of finish, however, can potentially make a difference in the instrument's sound. Most starter bass guitars have a polyurethane finish, although some higher-priced instruments have a lacquer or oil-based finish. No one finish is necessarily better than the others, and oil-based finishes often require more maintenance. Play several examples and see which one works best for you.

SHAPES AND SIZES

The shape of a bass guitar doesn't necessarily change the tone of the bass guitar, although it is an important factor in your comfort while playing. Several manufacturers have shapes traditionally associated with them, but it's up to you to determine which one works best for you. The size of a bass guitar can make a difference in the instrument's sound, as heavier instruments tend to resonate more than smaller ones, and make the notes ring longer. It can also affect how you play, as a heavier instrument may cause you fatigue and pain while playing. Take some time with each instrument and get a feel for its shape and weight before you buy.

THE PICKGUARD

Some bass guitar bodies have a piece of plastic near where the neck joins the body. This *pickguard* prevents excess wear or scratches to the body where people most often pluck the strings. It's not included on all bass guitar bodies; however, it can be helpful if you're playing an especially heavy type of music, such as punk or metal.

Pickguard

TIP

Be Comfortable!

Make sure your bass guitar's body is compatible with yours. Strange shapes or extremely heavy weights might make it difficult for you to play, so it's a good idea to stick to more traditional bodies when you're starting out.

The Neck

The neck of the bass is where the bassist actually chooses the notes being played. Most bass guitars have necks made of wood, although materials from aluminum to graphite have been used as well. The back of the neck is usually rounded; however, you might also encounter flattened or V-shaped necks as well.

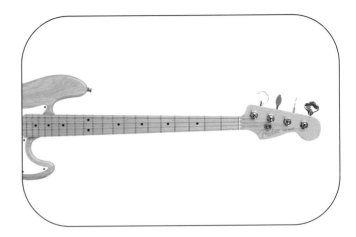

Neck Details

THE TRUSS ROD

The neck material itself must be strong enough to hold steady against the tension the strings create. In some cases, the wood may also have supports built in to keep it straight. A *truss rod* is essentially a large screw placed in the neck to allow more control over the straightness of the neck. The truss rod opening can be found either at the top or the bottom of the neck.

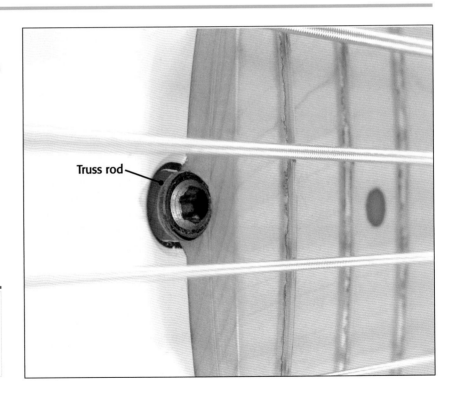

Truss rod

TIP

Don't Touch!
Only a qualified bass guitar technician should alter the truss rod of your instrument.

THE FINGERBOARD

The *fingerboard* of the neck is where your fingers and the strings actually meet the neck of the bass. The fingerboard is usually made of a different type of wood than the neck itself, based more on the tone the builder wants the bass to have.

TYPES OF FINGERBOARD WOOD

The two common types of wood are rosewood, which gives the bass a darker tone, and maple, which yields a brighter sound. Other exotic choices include ebony, pau ferro (commonly found in rain forests), and synthetic materials such as phenolic (a hard and durable resin). Some manufacturers inlay different-colored materials, like plastic or mother of pearl, at certain places on the fingerboard as position markers—visual cues to help players find notes.

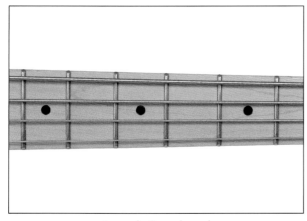

A maple fingerboard.

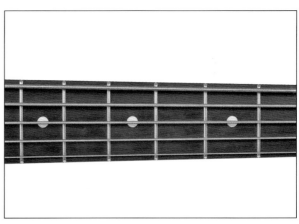

A rosewood fingerboard.

Fretted and Fretless Basses

There are two types of basses: those with fretted necks and those with fretless necks. Each have their own tonal properties that makes them valuable additions to your playing. This section discusses the difference between fretted and fretless bass guitars.

Types of Necks

FRETTED NECKS

The vast majority of starter bass guitars have fretted necks. *Frets* are metal strips or bands placed in the fingerboard. Each fret represents a note. When you hold down a string at a fret on the neck, the bass plays that note when plucked. The frets make sure that each note is the correct pitch when played.

Some bass guitars have *fretless* necks, where there are no frets in the fingerboard. It's more difficult to play correct pitches on these necks; however, fretless basses have a distinct sound, sometimes described as "mwah."

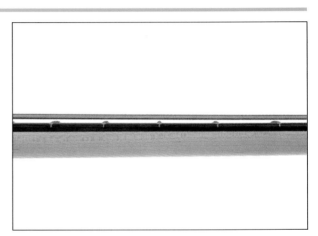

FRETLESS NECKS

Fretless necks come in two forms: *lined* and *unlined*. A lined fingerboard has lines drawn across it where the frets normally would be. By pressing down on the strings on those lines, the correct notes sound. Unlined fingerboards (as shown) look like the necks you might find on orchestral instruments such as the violin or cello. Only a trained ear and muscle memory will help you play in tune on unlined fingerboards.

For beginners, it's best to start on fretted instruments and try to tackle the fretless bass when you have a little more experience.

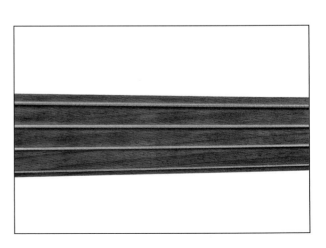

The Bridge

The bridge holds the strings to the body and plays an important role in keeping the strings in tune. It also helps set the level or height of the strings above the neck.

Bridge Details

The main function of the bridge is to anchor the strings to the body of the bass guitar. Additional screws and gears set the string height and the *intonation* of the bass guitar. By moving the bridge *saddles,* or the place where each string touches the bridge, a bass guitar technician can set the correct length between the nut and the bridge. That string length ensures that when the bass guitar is tuned, each note on the neck is correct.

Most bridges are made of metal. Some bass guitars have larger bridges with more metal, which increases the *sustain,* or the amount of time a note sounds when played.

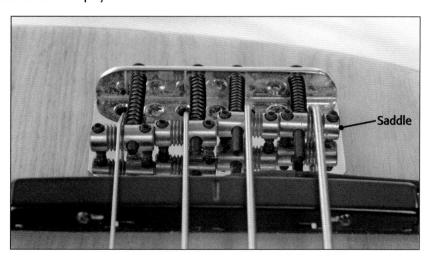

Saddle

 TIP

Cross That Bridge Later!
The bridge has several controls that require minute adjustments and attention to detail. It's better to leave these controls to the professionals.

Bass Guitar Strings

Bass guitar strings are fairly self-explanatory. The strings run from the head to the bridge, over the neck and the body. By holding a string down on the neck and plucking the string over the body, you play a note.

String Types

Bass guitar strings come in two main varieties: *roundwound* and *flatwound*. Roundwound strings are more common. Up close, they look like small, tightly coiled springs. Roundwounds are noted for their brighter, more sparkling tone. Flatwounds are flat on top, just as the name implies. Their tone is darker.

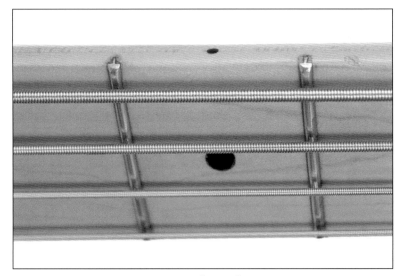

Roundwound

There is a dizzying variety of strings available, each promising to do a different thing better than the rest. Some even come in different colors or coated with special polymers or wound with tape. Let your ears tell you which ones to use. Roundwounds are usually more suited to most modern music—rock and other louder styles—whereas flatwounds might appeal more to jazz or classic R&B fans.

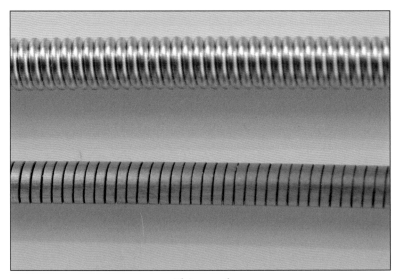

Flatwound

The original bass guitar came with four strings, just like the upright bass it was intended to sound like. As the instrument found its own unique identity, players and builders came up with the idea to put more strings on it. All of the examples in this book feature the 4-string bass because it's the most common model. Later, you can apply all the techniques you learn to the other strings.

More Than Four Strings

5-STRING BASS

The most common extended-range bass is the 5-string bass guitar (see photo). This adds a lower string to the normal bass guitar setup, allowing the bass guitar to play notes once reserved for the low end of the keyboard. Although the 5-string bass originally played the same role as bass parts played on keyboards in pop music during the 1980s, its lower notes also found popularity with modern metal players who sought lower, heavier sounds.

6-STRING BASS

Although not shown, another variety of bass guitar is the 6-string bass. It has as many strings as a normal guitar, but the extended upper and lower strings are tuned differently. Also, the extremely wide neck doesn't lend itself to playing chords very easily. This type of bass is preferred by soloists or jazz players looking for additional room to improvise.

Right-handed versus Left-handed Basses

Just like many players are right-handed, the majority of bass guitars are built "right-handed." That means the left hand is on the neck while the right hand is on the body.

Righties versus Lefties

However, some basses are built in the reverse direction, or "left-handed." In this case, the right hand holds the neck while the left hand rests on the body.

Some players might find that a left-handed bass feels more natural, and the examples in this book apply either way. I use the phrases "fretting hand" and "plucking hand" to avoid confusion. Still, you might find it easier to learn by playing right-handed. Give it a shot, and switch if it's giving you too many problems.

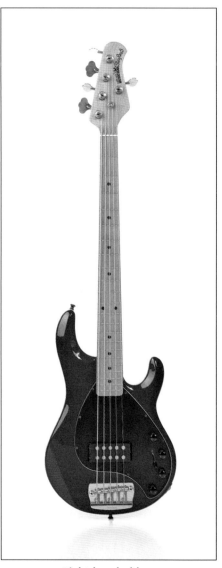

Right-handed bass

Left-handed bass

Think of the *pickups* on a bass as being like microphones. They "hear" and amplify the sound of the note produced by the bass guitar. The vibration of the string makes magnets in the pickup vibrate, creating an electrical signal that passes though the bass guitar to an amplifier.

Passive versus Active Pickups

Bass guitars can have one or more pickups, placed at various locations on the body. Each type is known for its different tone; however, they all fall into two main categories.

PASSIVE PICKUPS

These pickups are wired directly to the bass guitar's output jack and contain only basic controls, such as volume and tone. These are found on most older and classic bass guitars.

Passive pickups provide a sound true to the materials of the bass guitar, and some players prefer them to active pickups because of the warmer, more traditional sound they produce and their simple operations.

ACTIVE PICKUPS

These pickups are usually powered by a battery and include additional tone controls, much like the equalizer on your home stereo. These are usually louder than passive pickups, but you have to remember to change the battery.

Active pickups deliver more of a hi-fi sound, with access to a wider tonal spectrum than do passive pickups.

Depending on how many pickups your bass guitar has and whether they're active or passive, you'll have a variety of knobs and switches to learn.

Bass Guitar Controls

THE OUTPUT JACK

The one thing all basses have is the *output jack.* The output jack is where you plug in the cable that runs between your bass guitar and your amplifier. It's typically mounted on the body or the pickguard of the bass guitar.

Note: Output jacks can suffer from the stress of having a cord pulled too hard. Outputs mounted on the body or a metal pickguard are more stable than ones mounted on a plastic pickguard.

Jack

THE VOLUME KNOB

This knob controls the amount of volume the bass guitar puts out. Some bass guitars have only one volume control, whereas others have a separate volume knob for each pickup. This lets you blend the amount of volume from each pickup for different tone combinations.

THE TONE KNOB

This knob is found on passive bass guitars. It controls the amount of high frequencies sent to the amplifier. Keeping it all the way up makes the sound brighter, whereas turning it down gives it a deeper, darker quality.

EQ KNOBS

EQ (short for *equalization*) knobs are found on bass guitars with active pickups. Most EQ controls come with three different knobs: one for high frequencies, one for middle-range frequencies, and one for low frequencies.

PICKUP KNOBS AND SWITCHES

Bass guitars can also include knobs or switches that control which pickups are active. Switches move back and forth and turn pickups on or off.

Different combinations of pickups produce different tones. Combinations of pickups can also be controlled by *blend knobs.* At the middle position, both pickups are on equally. Turning the knob one way brings in one pickup more, whereas turning it the other way increases the other pickup.

chapter

3

Holding Your Bass Guitar

Before you can build a solid house, you have to start with a good foundation. Learning how to hold and play your bass guitar is the foundation you'll need to become a solid musician. This is where you start.

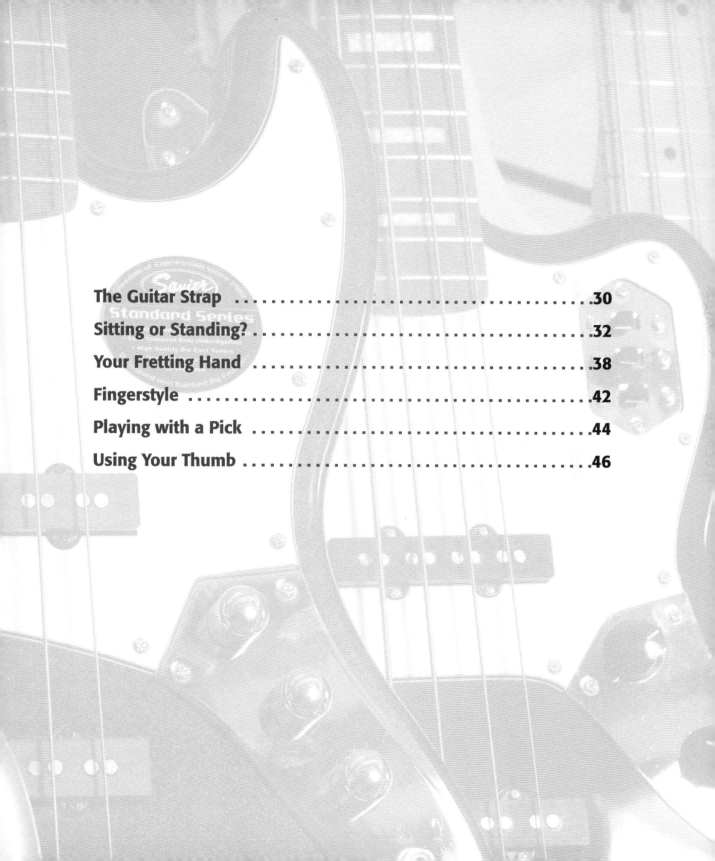

The Guitar Strap

Whether you're going to be playing sitting or standing, a guitar strap can help you maintain a good playing position and keep the instrument in the right place.

How to Attach the Strap

In most cases, the strap attaches to buttons on the back and the top horn of the bass guitar body. Different or extreme guitar body shapes could have different fastening areas. In this case, the strap is usually attached to the base of the neck and the back of the body. Either way works fine, as long as the buttons are solidly anchored to the body.

Some bass guitars also come with locking mechanisms that attach to the strap and lock to custom buttons on the bass guitar. You can buy these and attach them yourself as well.

TIP

Work Wood Wisely!

Be careful if you're removing screws from your bass guitar. If you strip the screw or the hole, it'll be difficult to get the screw to mount back in place once you're done.

HOW TO CHOOSE A STRAP

Choosing a strap is a matter of function and decoration. There are many custom guitar straps available in all manner of materials, from thin leather to thick, padded nylon mesh. If you have a particularly heavy bass guitar, it might be a good idea to invest in a wider, padded strap to help ease the weight and strain on your back. If this isn't a problem, let your imagination run wild.

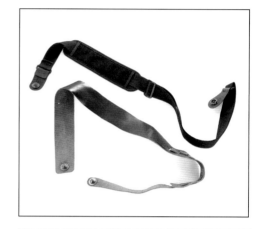

HOW TO WEAR A STRAP

The guitar strap should go over the shoulder of your fretting arm (left, for most people). You should then adjust the strap so that it's tight around your body, but not too tight. As you get more comfortable playing both seated and standing, you'll learn which strap length is right for you.

TIP

Change It!
Changing the strap length between sitting and standing helps you keep your bass guitar at the right position.

Sitting or Standing?

Before you can play bass guitar, every part of your body must be comfortable and relaxed. Whether you've taken a seat or are standing on stage, your hands and arms must be able to move around the bass guitar easily and without undue stress. Make sure your wrists are straight at all times. This will help you not only move around the guitar easier, but also avoid stress and pain down the road.

The Sitting Position

Let's start with the proper sitting position to play bass guitar:

1. Make sure you're sitting on a chair or bench without arms. That way, you can hold the bass guitar in the proper position without hitting any part of the furniture.

2. You can either keep both feet flat on the floor or cross your legs, depending on your comfort level.

3. Rest the body of the bass guitar on your right leg (left leg if you're playing left-handed).

④ Keep the fretboard at a 90-degree angle to the floor or slightly inclined toward your body.

⑤ Put your right arm over the body of the bass, with your right hand near the strings.

⑥ Hold the neck with your left hand near the head.

TIP

Take a Break!
If you notice any pain or stress in your fingers while you're playing, take a break and shake it off. It's important that you don't hurt yourself during the learning process.

CONTINUED ON NEXT PAGE

YOUR BASS MIGHT AFFECT YOUR POSITION

Depending on the shape of your bass guitar, you might have to alter this position slightly. The more conventional body types have indentions in the body that allow you to comfortably rest the instrument on your leg. Extreme custom shapes or a flat bottom might cause problems with balance.

Additionally, an extremely heavy head might cause the bass guitar to dip. Again, slight adjustments are okay, but it's important to maintain the basic form so that your arms and hands have easy access to the strings.

THE "SITTING" ARM AND WRIST POSITION

You should always keep your wrists straight in the seated position. See how you should hold your arms to keep your wrists in the proper position. Your fretting hand wrist should be as straight as possible with your arm (as seen in the top photo on this page), as should your right wrist (as seen in the bottom photo). Your goal should be to keep your wrists as straight as possible to allow a full range of motion without cramping or hurting your hands.

CONTINUED ON NEXT PAGE

The Standing Position

The guitar strap mentioned earlier is an important part of playing while standing. The strap should take all of the weight of the bass guitar, leaving your hands free to move without supporting the instrument. It should also be positioned high enough so that you can keep your wrists straight while playing. The top photo shows the proper standing position. The bottom photo shows an improper standing position.

The "Standing" Arm and Wrist Position

Notice how the only part of the arms that are bent are the elbows. Every other joint, especially the wrists, should be straight.

Make sure you keep your strap high enough to properly position your hands and arms. Avoid keeping the bass so low that your wrists bend awkwardly. This creates unnecessary stress and could lead to problems down the road. Your fretting hand elbow should be pointing towards the floor, while your plucking hand elbow should be pointed off to the side.

Fretting is the act of holding down a note on the neck of the bass guitar; thus, your *fretting hand* is the one that holds down the notes. This most likely is your left hand, although some players using left-handed basses use their right hand. To avoid confusion, we'll use the term "fretting hand" throughout this book.

Thumb Placement

Although it never touches the strings, your thumb is an important part of moving your hand around and shifting over the strings. It acts almost like a pivot or a hinge, keeping its place while the fingers move around its support (a).

You'll be tempted at several points during your playing to hook your thumb over the neck of the bass guitar (b). This makes it more difficult to properly fret notes with your fingers. Be sure to always keep your thumb on the back of the neck. Your playing and range of motion benefit greatly from proper placement.

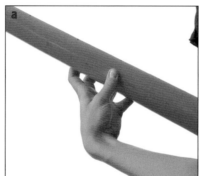

1. Position your thumb flat on the back of the neck.

2. Make sure your wrist remains straight.

3. Try moving your fingers over the strings without actually holding any down. First pivot your hand to your left (a) while keeping your thumb in place, and then move it to the right (b). Get used to the feeling of your hand moving around the fulcrum of your thumb.

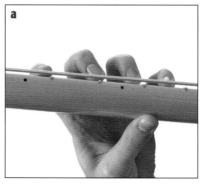

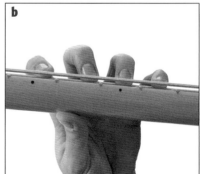

Hand Placement

Now that you've got your thumb anchored on the back of the neck, let's look at the fingers on the front of the neck. When you first start playing, make sure that the fingers fall on the neck with the thumb between the middle and ring fingers.

Again, move your hand around with the thumb in its proper place, but concentrate on your fingers this time. Notice the amount of space your hand can cover in this position.

Now try moving your hand up and down from the lowest string to the highest string, again keeping your thumb placed on the back of the neck.

This method allows you a great deal of motion around the neck without moving your hand too much. This eventually gives you a smooth and natural feel in your playing.

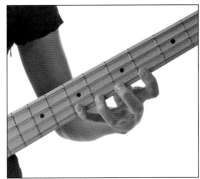

CONTINUED ON NEXT PAGE

Your Fingers

Now that your hand and thumb are in the right place, take a look at your fingers. When you're fretting a note, your finger should be slightly curved, and only the tip of your finger should be touching the string.

It might hurt a little bit at first, but eventually you'll build up calluses that will eliminate the pain.

1 Slightly curve your index finger, as shown in the photo.

2 Place the tip of your finger directly behind the fret of the note you're going to play.

3 Press down on the note using only the pad of your finger.

Again, it's going to seem easier at first to just curl your hand around the neck of the bass. This prevents you from moving your hand quickly around the neck, causing problems with your playing. It could also make it more difficult to keep your wrist straight. Both of these photos show an incorrect playing style.

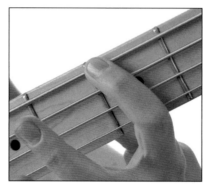

Correct placement of index finger

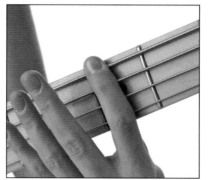

Incorrect placement of index finger

TIP

Off the Top!
Do not try to hold down the note directly on top of the fret. You'll hear some buzzing, and it's more likely that your finger will slip off.

As you practice fretting notes, try to do it with each of your fingers. Yes, you'll even practice with your pinky finger. All of your fingers play an equal role when it comes to fretting notes. You might have some difficulty at first because your fingers will be unused to the positioning and strength necessary to hold down a note. Again, this is something that goes away as you build strength and calluses on your fingers. Practice each finger individually, keeping in mind the correct playing position:

1 Keep your wrist straight.

2 Keep your thumb solidly in the middle of the neck.

3 Keep your fingers slightly curved.

4 Press down only with the tips of your fingers.

5 Press down on the string directly behind the fret of the note you want to play.

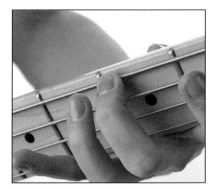

Correct middle finger placement

Correct ring finger placement

Correct pinky finger placement

Fingerstyle

The preceding section dealt with your fretting hand, so let's take a look at your *plucking hand*. You might also hear it called your *picking hand*, depending on the style you use to actually cause the note to sound. This chapter introduces you to the finger-style method of plucking the strings.

Plucking

As opposed to a guitar, where the player strums the strings, a bassist is more likely to pluck the strings one at a time, using an upward motion. The most common way to do this involves the index and middle fingers.

1. Extend the index and middle fingers on your plucking hand.

2. Fold your ring and pinky fingers into your palm. If that doesn't feel comfortable, you can let your fingers hang down, but keep them out of the way of the strings.

3. Place your index and middle fingers over the strings, perpendicular to the length of the strings. It's a good idea to anchor your thumb on the body of the bass, a pickup, or the *E* string when it's not being played.

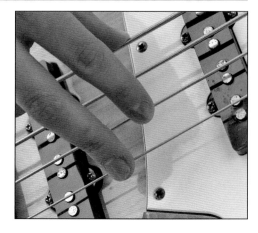

4. Rest only the pads of your index and middle fingers on the strings. If you place more than that on the strings, it can keep the notes from ringing.

5 Pluck a string softly using the pad of your index finger, making a note. Let your plucking finger come to rest on the next string down.

6 Now pluck a string with the pad of your middle finger, making a note.

This is another instance in which building up your calluses helps. You want to pluck with enough force to make a note, but not so hard that you cause loud buzzing or clacking. Eventually, you'll learn the proper amount of force to use to play in every situation, from quiet passages to loud, aggressive rock.

Some players also include their ring and pinky fingers in the plucking motion, but it's best to master using your index and middle fingers first before moving on.

Alternating Your Fingers

Once you've learned how to pluck with both your index and middle fingers, it's time to alternate them. This method of plucking enables you to play a note and have the next finger ready to pluck. This means you'll be able to increase the speed at which you can play. Ultimately, you'll want to make both fingers sound strong and clear.

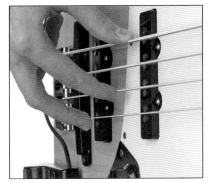

I talk more in depth about fingerstyle playing in Chapter 6; however, the important thing to get used to now is the feeling of plucking the strings with your fingers. Although some players use a pick, finger plucking is the most common way to play bass guitar.

This is one playing style that is common to both guitar and bass guitar. A *pick* or *plectrum* is a small piece of plastic, metal, or other material held in the hand and used to strike the string of the bass guitar. This produces a harder sound than fingerstyle, so it's often favored by louder or more aggressive styles of music, such as hard rock, metal, or punk.

Pick Types and Instruction

If you've played guitar before, you might have played with a thin pick made for strumming smaller strings. For bass strings, you'll find that thicker picks produce clearer tones and react better to the larger strings. Thinner picks don't have the strength to play easily on bass strings.

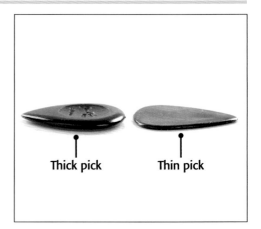

Thick pick   Thin pick

Follow these steps to pick a downstroke on a bass guitar:

1. Hold the pick between your index finger and your thumb.

2. Place the tip of the pick just over the string you want to play.

3. Bring the pick down and strike the string. Use your wrist to start the picking motion, not your fingers.

4. Follow through with the pick, stopping before you hit the next string.

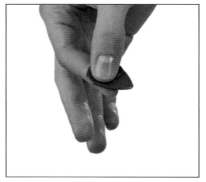

Types of Picking

There are two main types of picking on the bass guitar, alternate picking (shown in top photo) and downpicking (shown in bottom photo).

ALTERNATE PICKING

Alternate picking involves the use of an upstroke following the down-stroke described earlier in this section. Just bring your pick up using your wrist and strike the string again.

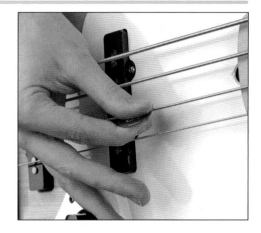

DOWNPICKING

This involves the use of only down strokes. Instead of hitting the string on the way back up, you just bring the pick up and play another downstroke. Although this isn't the fastest way to play at the beginning, some players favor it because they believe the downstroke produces a richer, harder, and potentially a more even tone. With practice, some players can down-pick as fast as alternate pickers.

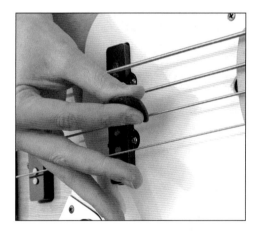

TIP

Try It Both Ways

There are advantages to both fingerstyle and pick-playing techniques. You'll probably find you favor one over the other eventually, but give both a chance and you'll have more tonal options available when you play.

There are two styles of creating notes using the thumb on your plucking hand. The first involves using your thumb much like a pick. Players using this technique often want a deeper, warmer tone than they usually get using their fingers or a pick. This can be especially helpful in styles such as folk or country music, where the bass guitar is expected to provide a solid bass note and not much else.

Some older bass guitars actually have small bars at the bottom of the body to place your fingers on while you use your thumb to pluck notes. If you don't have one of these, just rest the tips of your fingers on the body just after the last string. Be sure you don't touch the strings themselves—you want to let the notes ring.

1 Place your thumb on the string you're going to play.

2 Bring your thumb down to strike the string.

3 Continue the motion as your thumb slides over the string to produce the note.

4 Put your thumb on the same string or the string you're going to play next.

5 Continue this motion throughout the song.

For a slightly muted sound, you can also try this motion at the back of the body while resting your palm on the bridge of the bass guitar.

This placement tends to keep the notes from ringing out as long. In some cases, such as a traditional country song with a strong emphasis on a "two-beat" feel, deadening the notes more quickly puts more space between notes, giving the song more "room to breathe." As you move your palm farther up the strings, you use a technique called *palm muting*. Palm muting gives the note a more thumping tone with less length. It's also useful to help simulate a sound similar to synthesized keyboard bass, giving the notes a low thump.

When somebody in the group yells "Break it down!", that might be a good time to use this technique.

CONTINUED ON NEXT PAGE

Slapping and Popping

Slapping and popping, or just *slap bass,* is one of the most unique ways to play the bass guitar. Invented by Sly and the Family Stone bassist Larry Graham in the '70s and made popular by bassists ranging from Bootsy Collins to Flea and Victor Wooten, slapping is a high-energy and extremely noticeable technique for playing both rhythm and solo parts.

HOW TO SLAP

The trick is to know exactly when to do it. Because it is so high-energy, it might sound out of place in a slow ballad or folk song. Slapping usually takes place in funk or pop tunes, although it has made its presence felt in rock and metal to an extent.

Slapping is very descriptive of the actual technique. The player slaps the string with the thumb, causing a loud strike. The popping comes from looping your index finger under a string and pulling it up, causing the note to sound with a snapping tone. Needless to say, this is a very physical style of playing.

1. Stick your thumb out, in a hitchhiking motion.
2. Curl your other fingers into your palm, except for the index finger.
3. Place your thumb over the string you're going to play.
4. Using your wrist, bring your thumb down on the string.
5. Twist your wrist to bring your thumb back quickly, like you were using a doorknob.

Slapping is a percussive attack, like a drumstick hitting a drum. Keep that motion in mind as you play.

HOW TO POP

1. To pop the string, loop your index finger under a string.
2. Pull the string up slightly with your index finger.
3. Release the string from your first finger, causing the string to snap back against the neck and body.

Be careful when you're starting out with this technique. It's easy to break the strings by pulling or hitting them too hard. The trick is to use just enough power to get the sound without causing a lot of damage to the strings. They're more resilient than you might think, though.

I cover more slapping in Chapter 11. Until then, practice the basics for this technique, but use fingerstyle and picking for the examples you see later in the book. You'll probably end up using those playing styles more, anyway, as they are more commonly what people look for in a supportive bass player.

chapter 4

Tuning Your Bass Guitar

Before playing, you've got to make sure everything will sound right. Tuning your bass guitar means adjusting the basic pitch of the strings correctly so that every note will be correct and in tune. Not only will the bass guitar be tuned correctly to itself, but you'll be able to play in tune with other instruments, such as guitars or keyboards.

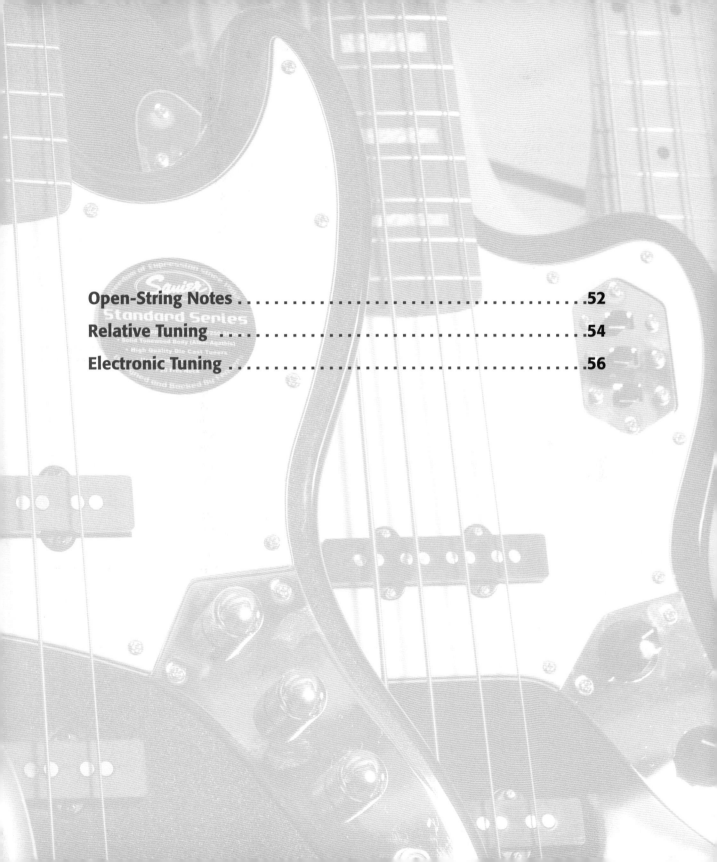

Open-String Notes

When you play a string without fretting a note, this is called an *open* note or string. Each string is tuned to a specific note—from lowest pitch to highest pitch, the strings are tuned to the notes *E, A, D,* and *G.* Physically, the string closest to your face is the E string, and the pitches get higher as you move towards the strings closer to the ground.

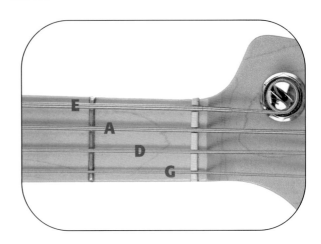

Tune with the Gears

You use the tuning gears on the head of the bass guitar to tighten or loosen the strings and bring them to the correct pitch. When a string is out of tune, it's either *sharp* (the note is too high) or *flat* (the note is too low). Tightening up the string causes the note to move up, whereas loosening it causes it to go down.

In most cases, if the tuning gears are on the top of the head (a), turning the tuning gears clockwise tunes them up by tightening the strings. Turning them counterclockwise tunes the strings down by loosening them.

If some or all of the tuning gears are on the bottom of the head (b), meaning they point at the ground, the opposite is true for the bottom tuning gears. Turning them clockwise tunes the strings down (loosening them) and turning them counterclockwise tunes the strings up (tightening them).

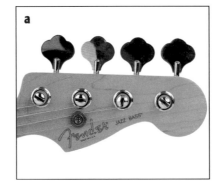

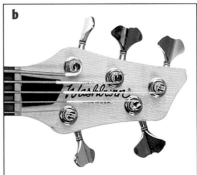

Methods of Tuning

Two methods are used to get your bass guitar into tune. You can either tune each string to another instrument, such as a keyboard or an electronic tuner; or you can tune one string of the bass guitar and then tune the remaining strings to it. The latter method is called relative tuning and is discussed on the following page.

In any case, it's vital that you tune the bass guitar every time before you play. When you're first developing your ear for playing a new instrument, you need to make sure that you're hearing everything accurately. Practicing out of tune only reinforces bad tones and bad habits.

Although you should tune every time before you play, you shouldn't have to tune up much more than that. If your bass guitar won't stay in tune, try changing the strings. Older strings are often too fatigued to hold their tune. (I talk more about changing strings in Chapter 14.) If this continues, you might have to have a repair specialist (often called a luthier) examine the tuning gears and bridge.

Also, make sure that you never tune the strings on your bass guitar too high for long periods of time. This can put too much strain on both the string and the neck, resulting in a bent or twisted neck.

TIP

Moving On Up!

It's always a good idea to tune up to the note, rather than tune down to the note—that is, tightening the string to reach the correct pitch as opposed to loosening it. This helps the gears grip the string, making sure it stays in pitch longer. If your string is sharp, tune down to below the note and then tune up to the correct pitch.

Relative Tuning

Take a look at relative tuning, or tuning the strings on your bass guitar to one common string. This is a quick and easy way to get every string in tune with the others. The key here is to make sure that you tune one string first, and then tune all of the other strings in relation to it. The tuning for the original string should stay in place.

How to Tune Using Relative Pitch

You can tune any string on the bass guitar first and use it as your reference pitch; however, a common choice is tuning the *A* string first. *A* is the note that large ensembles usually tune to, and it's often available as a reference pitch on other electronic devices such as a metronome.

To tune a bass guitar using relative pitch, perform the following steps:

1. Match the pitch of the *A* string on the bass guitar to an *A* on an external source, such as a keyboard or the reference tone on a tuner. If the string's pitch is below this external pitch, tune it up. If the string is too high, loosen it to below the external pitch and then tune it up.

2. Hold the *E* string down on the 5th fret (see photo). This should be the same pitch as the *A* string.

3. Play the *E* string with the note held down and the *A* string at the same time. If the *E* string sounds lower than the *A* string, tune it up to match the *A* string's pitch. If the *E* string is too high, tune it below the *A* string and then bring it up to tune.

④ Hold down the 5th fret on the *A* string (see photo). This should be the same pitch as the open *D* string just above it.

⑤ Play the *A* string with the note held down and the *D* string at the same time. This time, however, you're tuning the open *D* string and not the *A* string. If the *D* string sounds lower than the *A* string, tune it up to match the *A* string's pitch. If the *D* string is too high, tune it below the *A* string and then bring it up to tune.

⑥ When you're sure those strings are in tune, hold down the 5th fret on the *D* string (see photo). This should be the same pitch as the open *G* string.

⑦ Play the *D* string with the note held down and the open *G* string at the same time. If the open *G* string sounds lower than the *D* string, tune it up to match the *D* string's pitch. If the *G* string is too high, tune it below the *D* string and then bring it up to tune.

By the time you're finished with this, your bass guitar will be in tune. This example also brings up a useful fact about the bass guitar: *In standard tuning, the 5th fret on the string is always the same pitch as the open string just above it.* Keep this in mind because it will be useful later in the book.

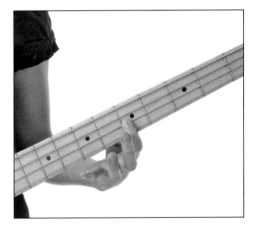

FAQ

How can I tell if my bass guitar is out of tune?

Strings that are dramatically out of tune will be obvious to your ear; however, closer pitches can sometimes be confusing. You might hear a "beating" sound or a rhythmic pulse when you play two of the same notes together that aren't in tune with one another. The effect you're hearing is the vibrations of the strings interfering with each other.

The trick here is to tune so that the pulse slows to a stop. Turn the tuning gears slowly until the beating sound slows down, then goes away.

Electronic Tuning

An electronic tuner is valuable for several reasons. First, because you can usually connect a bass guitar directly to an electronic tuner, you can tune up in louder situations in which you might not be able to hear everything correctly (such as when all of your bandmates are tuning up at the same time). You can also tune silently, without bothering anybody else with the noise. Finally, whether you connect directly to the tuner or the tuner uses a small microphone to "hear" your pitch, you won't need an outside, or external, pitch to tune to. The electronic tuner takes care of it all.

How to Tune with an Electronic Tuner

Some tuners are small, handheld models that can pick up both ambient sound and direct connections to the bass guitar (see a). Tuner pedals (see b) accept only direct connections, but also mute the signal so that nobody can hear you tune—a considerate move for your audience. Finally, rackmount tuners reside in the same enclosure as your amplifier for ease of transport.

Note: *Most electronic tuners display not only the notes of the open string, but also some kind of visual representation to show how far above or below the correct pitch the string is. This helps you see where the string's pitch is and whether you need to tune up or down.*

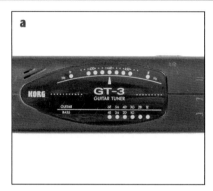

Hand-held tuner

Tuner pedal

To tune the bass guitar using an electronic tuner, perform the following steps:

1 Connect the tuner to your bass guitar with a cable, or put the tuner next to the bass guitar amplifier.

2 Turn the tuner on.

3 Play the *E* string on the bass guitar and look at the readout on the tuner.

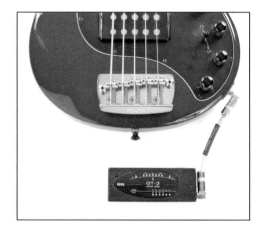

④ If the readout shows the string as being too low, or flat, tune the *E* string up. Keep plucking the string as you tune. Notice how the readout changes as you tune it up.

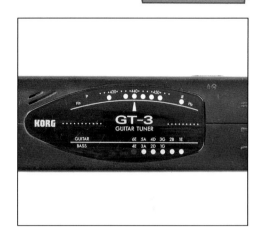

⑤ If the *E* string is too high, or sharp, tune the *E* string to below the correct pitch and tune up. Follow step 4 from here.

⑥ Repeat these steps for each of the other strings.

⑦ When everything is in tune, go back and play each of the strings again, checking their tuning one last time. Tuning other strings might have thrown something off slightly. If a string does need retuning, it should just be by a small amount.

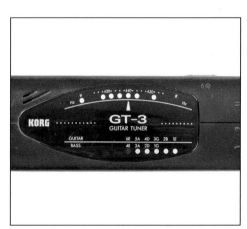

TIP

Electronic or Relative Tuning?

Although it's handy to have an electronic tuner around, it's a good idea to learn how to tune your bass guitar by ear using relative tuning as well. Not only does it get your ear used to hearing the correct pitches for each string, but it also helps you tune to other instruments or deal with the situation of a dead battery in your tuner. It happens to everybody at some point.

5

Basic Fretboard Fingering

This chapter helps you build the finger independence and strength necessary to play in all positions along the fingerboard. You'll learn how to properly fret a note with each finger on your hand and how to move your fingers up and down the neck quickly and easily. You'll also learn how to keep your hand in the proper position to play the notes more quickly without your fingers leaving the fretboard.

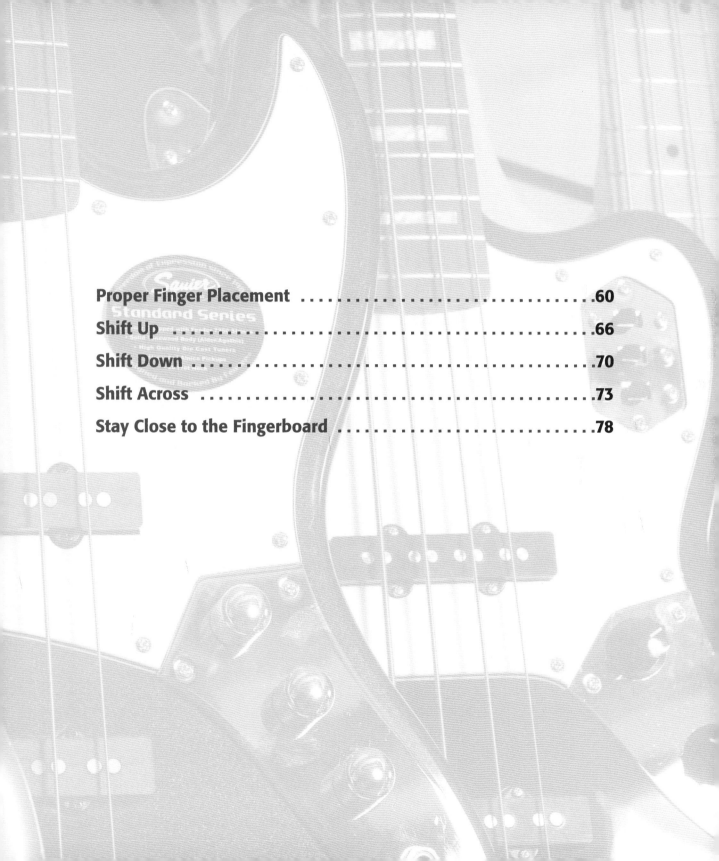

Proper Finger Placement

Proper finger placement means that you can easily and swiftly reach any position on the fretboard with a minimum of time and effort. You want to give yourself the opportunity to play whatever you need, whenever you need, without having to shift your hand too much. Proper placement will help you do this.

Before You Play

REMEMBER: ONE FINGER PER FRET

You already saw the proper way to fret a note, or hold down a note on the neck, in Chapter 3. So you know that you need to hold down the note just behind the fret with the tip of your finger, keeping the finger itself slightly curved. You also know that you're supposed to use every finger on your fretting hand to play notes, including the pinky.

This is the introduction to a very important concept: using one finger per fret. This allows you to cover the maximum amount of notes with your fretting hand without having to shift your hand up or down the neck. This will help your playing be more even and consistent.

WARM UP

Before beginning the exercises in this chapter (or before any extended playing, really), it's a good idea to warm up your hands. Just like a runner stretches his or her legs before going for a jog to prevent cramps, you need to exercise your fingers before you get down to business to prevent cramping or straining.

A common first step is just to shake your hands for a minute or two. This gets the blood flowing and loosens up your muscles. You can also close and open your fingers into a fist repeatedly for a few minutes. Don't squeeze too tightly, but keep the fingers moving. Finally, when you do start playing, start slowly and work your way up to higher speeds. I'll talk more about using a metronome for precise times in Chapter 10. For now, though, just remember to play each note slowly and deliberately at first, and speed up gradually as you go along and get more comfortable.

Finger Exercises

Here are some exercises to help you build the strength in your fingers and make them more independent.

① Using your index finger, hold down the 5th fret on the *E* string (see photo). Again, this note is an *A*.

② Pluck the note and let the *A* ring.

③ Using your middle finger, fret the 6th fret on the *E* string (see photo). This note is a *B flat*.

④ Pluck the note and let the *B flat* ring.

⑤ Remove your middle finger from the *B flat,* leaving your index finger on the *A*.

⑥ Repeat this process several more times until you become comfortable with the process and each note rings clearly, without any buzzing.

Notice how you never remove your index finger from the *A* the entire time. Fretting the *B flat* means you won't hear the *A*, but keeping your finger there means you're prepared to play that *A* much more easily.

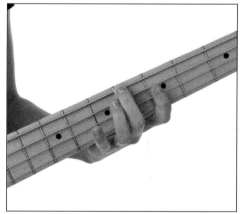

Now, try the same thing with your index and ring fingers.

① Hold down the *A* on the *E* string with your index finger.

② Pluck the note and let the *A* ring.

③ Keeping your index finger in place, hold down the 7th fret on the *E* string with your ring finger (see photo). This note is a *B*.

④ Pluck the note and let the *B* ring.

⑤ Remove your middle finger from the *B*, leaving your index finger on the *A*.

⑥ Repeat this process several more times until you become comfortable with the process and each note rings clearly, without any buzzing.

CONTINUED ON NEXT PAGE

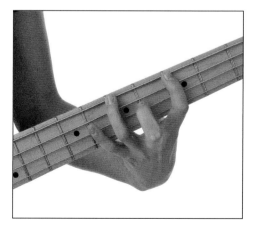

You might feel some strain in your left hand with the last exercise. Your fingers are required to make a little more of a stretch with the following exercise, which works on the pinky finger. It might feel the most unnatural of all the finger exercises presented here, just because you don't use your pinky independently of your other fingers that often. The pinky needs to hold its own in playing notes, though, so make sure you train it right.

1. Hold down the *A* on the *E* string with your index finger.

2. Pluck the note and let the *A* ring.

3. Using your pinky finger, fret the 8th fret on the *E* string (see photo). This note is a *C*.

4. Pluck the note and let the *C* ring.

5. Remove your middle finger from the *C,* leaving your index finger on the *A*.

6. Repeat this process several more times until you become comfortable with the process and each note rings clearly, without any buzzing.

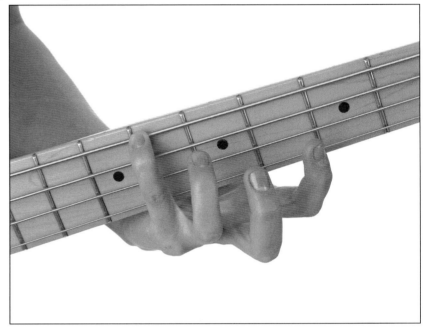

You'll probably feel some strain with this exercise initially, and you might not be able to hold down the *A* and the *C* at the same time as you did in the earlier examples. That's okay; it will take some time to get your fingers used to performing this action. The important thing is to keep trying to make the stretch as you go on. Even if it doesn't happen immediately, it will happen.

TIP

Warming Up

Start each of these exercises slowly to warm up. Your fingers will loosen up and move easier, and you'll find that you can play better as you go along. Slight finger stretching and wiggling will also assist your warm ups.

You can add some more fingers to the exercises. Remember to keep your fingers down unless you have to lift them to let the next note play.

1 Hold down the *A* on the *E* string with your index finger.

2 Pluck the note and let the *A* ring.

3 Hold down the *B flat* on the *E* string with your middle finger.

4 Pluck the note and let the *B flat* ring.

5 Hold down the *B* on the *E* string with your ring finger.

6 Pluck the note and let the *B* ring.

7 Hold down the *C* on the *E* string with your pinky finger (see photo). Remember to meanwhile continue holding down *A*, *B flat*, and *B*.

8 Pluck the note and let the *C* ring.

9 Lift your pinky finger and pluck the *B*. Let the note ring.

10 Lift your ring finger and pluck the *B flat*. Let the note ring.

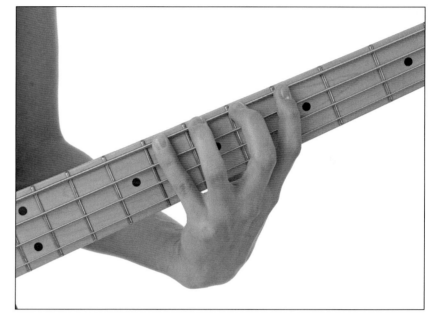

11 Lift your middle finger and pluck the *A*. Let the note ring.

12 Repeat this process several more times until you become comfortable with the process and each note rings clearly, without any buzzing.

Again, don't worry if you can't make these stretches immediately. They'll come to you with practice.

That's also the reason this exercise is located toward the middle of the neck, so that you won't get discouraged by trying these stretches on the lower notes, where there's more space between frets. As you get more comfortable with these exercises, try moving them closer to the nut. Again, take it slow and remember to stretch.

CONTINUED ON NEXT PAGE

Proper Finger Placement (continued)

The following charts show you examples of how to fret these notes in a different order each time. The number indicates the order in which you should play the notes, and the correct fingering (index, middle, ring, pinky) is written next to each note. With each exercise, start slowly and build up the speed as you get more comfortable. Eventually, you'll want to be able to play any possible combination of these notes, keeping your fingers from moving from their assigned frets:

    1st fret = index finger (i)
    2nd fret = middle finger (m)
    3rd fret = ring finger (r)
    4th fret = pinky finger (p)

From here, you can work on this exercise with the notes in a different order. Try using the following finger combinations:

1234	2341
1324	3142
1423	3214
2413	4132
2314	4231

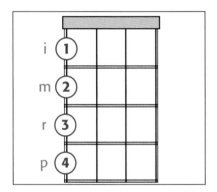
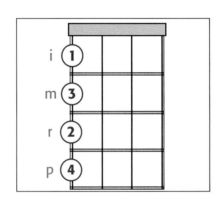
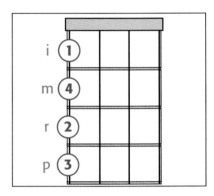
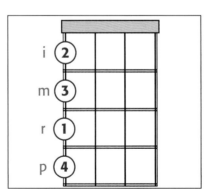
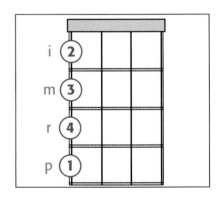

These combinations will help you build both finger strength and independence. You'll find it easier to play faster and more complicated music if your fingers are able to move independently of your other fingers, and the increased strength with help your notes sound better. Make this a part of your normal warm-up and practice, and you'll notice a big difference as you go on.

This exercise helps your fingers move independently of each other, and it also teaches you to cover the largest amount of notes possible in each hand position. Repeat these combinations on the remaining strings.

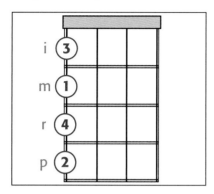

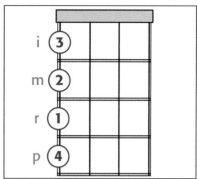

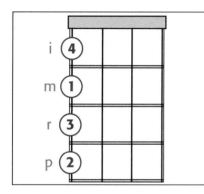

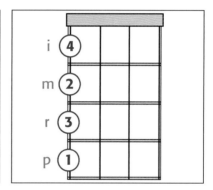

Shift Up

In shifting up, your goal is to move smoothly up to the higher position and play the part as cleanly as possible. You'll know you've shifted correctly when you don't notice any difference in the notes from one position to the next.

Upshift Exercises

Part of the hand positioning you've looked at up to this point in this book is meant to keep your hand from moving too much. As a bassist, it's important to make every note clear and defined. Shifting your hand around too much can detract from that goal. Sometimes, however, you just have to move your hand around. The song you're playing might require notes at various points along the fretboard, or you might want to hit a high note for special effect.

Take the exercise from earlier in this chapter and move it up and down the fretboard to get comfortable with shifting.

1. Starting on *A* on the *E* string (the 5th fret on the lowest string), play the *A* through the *C* notes using the one-finger-per-fret method.

2. Before playing the *C* note with your pinky, lift up your other fingers in a smooth motion (see photo). Keep them close to the fingerboard, but don't touch the string.

3. After playing the *C* note and letting it ring, hold down the *B flat* (the 6th fret on the *E* string) with your index finger (see photo).

4. In a smooth motion, let your thumb slide forward just a little bit and let your fingers move to the next fret up from where they were. The index finger moves to *B flat,* the middle finger to *B,* and so on.

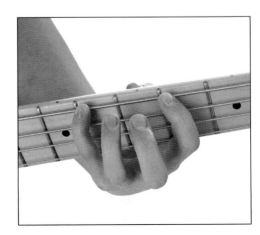

⑤ Play each note beginning with your index finger on the *B flat* (see photo).

⑥ Repeat this process as you move up the neck. Remember to let your thumb slide up slowly each time and keep it on the center of the back of the neck.

This is a subtle and slight way to change positions. If you're moving up the neck in small amounts of space, this keeps your notes sounding clean and clear without much shifting effort.

Now look at a way to make more dramatic shifts up the neck.

① Using the one-finger-per-fret method, play the *A* through the *C* notes on the *E* string.

② Again, as you play the *C* note on the *E* string with your pinky, lift your fingers in a smooth motion, keeping them close to the fingerboard.

③ This time, however, move your index finger to the *B* note on the *E* string.

④ Let your thumb slide down the neck in a smooth motion and let your fingers fall into their new position as you once again follow the one-finger-per-fret technique.

⑤ Play each note beginning with your index finger on the *B* (see photo).

⑥ Repeat this process as you move up the neck. Remember to let your thumb slide slowly up each time and keep it on the center of the back of the neck.

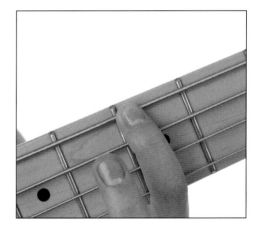

This shift was a little more dramatic, but it still emphasized moving the hand smoothly in a small increment.

CONTINUED ON NEXT PAGE

TIP

Keep the noise down!
Part of a smooth shift is a minimum of string noise. You shouldn't hear a lot of squeaks or scratches as you move your fretting hand around. You'll know you're shifting correctly when you don't hear a lot of extra noise.

Now, take a look at moving the hand to a completely new position in one motion.

1. Play the *A* through *C* notes on the *E* string using the one-finger-per-fret method.

2. After playing the *C* note, smoothly move your hand in one motion up the neck so that the index finger lands on the 8th fret of the *E* string, or *D flat* (see photo)—the note just above where your pinky just played the *C*.

3. Repeat this motion farther up on the *E* string, beginning on the *D flat*.

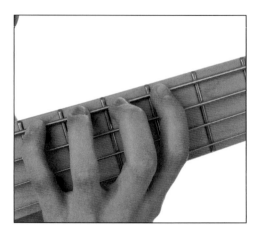

This represents a dramatic shift of hand position, but notice that it accomplished the task of moving your hand in one smooth motion. Once you made that motion, you had the full range of your fingers available again. Again, the fewer times you have to shift your hand, the more consistent and even your sound is. You also have less hand fatigue and stress as you play.

TIP

For now, keep in mind that shifts should always be smooth, accurate, and transparent. That is, do everything in a calm and deliberate manner, land in the right places, and make sure that the shift doesn't affect the sound of the notes you play. If you hear any buzzing or rattling, slow down and make sure you get it right before speeding up.

The following diagrams show where on the fretboard you should play the notes, and where you should end up after you make the shift. Use these as an example, and make sure your shifts are strong and smooth.

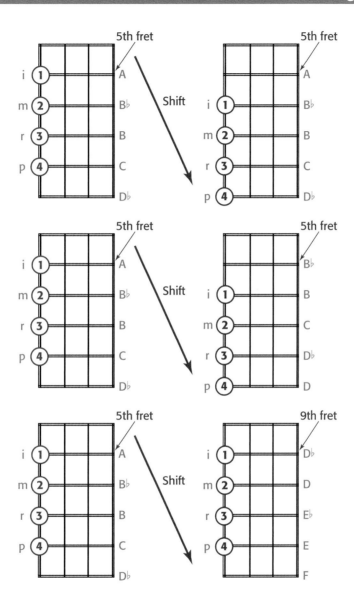

In a lot of ways, shifting your fretting hand down the neck is the same as shifting your hand up the neck. It just goes in a different direction. The same one-finger-per-fret technique still applies, and you still want to make sure all of your shifts are smooth, accurate, and transparent.

Downshift Exercises

With that said, look at the technical side of shifting down the neck.

Start with your fingers in the same position as in the previous exercises. Your index finger should be on the *A* note on the *E* string, your middle finger on the *B flat*, and so on. In this case, however, start playing the notes beginning with the *C*, the note your pinky is fretting.

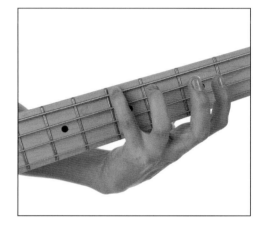

1. Play the *C* note fretted by the pinky on the *E* string (the 8th fret on the *E* string).

2. Play the rest of the notes descending the neck in the order of *B, B flat*, and *A*.

3. As you play the *A* note with your index finger, move your pinky to the *B* on the *E* string (the 7th fret).

4. Fret the *B* with your pinky (see photo).

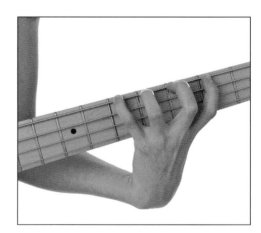

5. Slide your thumb slightly down the back of the neck of the bass and allow your fingers to fall in the frets behind the *B*. Your ring finger should be on the *B flat*, your middle finger should be on the *A*, and your index finger should be on the note just below the *A*, on the 4th fret, called the *A flat* (see photo).

6. Play the notes from *B* to *A flat*.

7. Repeat this exercise down to the bottom of the neck toward the headstock.

The mechanics of this shift are the same as shifting up, except that you're beginning your playing on the pinky and shifting down the neck. You might also notice that you're stretching a little bit more as you move down due to the space between the frets. Keep in mind that you always need to fret the notes directly behind the fret. Keep trying for the proper stretch; it will come through practice.

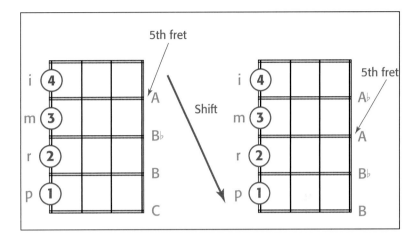

Try increasing the amount of shift again. Start in the same position as in the preceding exercise, but you're going to be moving your hand a little more this time.

1 Play the C note fretted by the pinky on the E string at the 8th fret.

2 Play the rest of the notes going down the neck in order of *B, B flat,* and *A.*

3 As you play the *A* note with your index finger, move your pinky to the *B flat* on the *E* string.

4 Fret the *B flat* with your pinky (see photo).

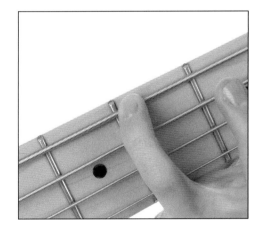

5 Slide the thumb slightly down the back of the neck of the bass and allow your fingers to fall in the frets behind the *B flat* (see photo). Your ring finger should be on the *A,* your middle finger should be on the *A flat,* and your index finger should be on the note just below the *A flat,* called the *G.*

6 Play the notes from *B flat* to *G.*

CONTINUED ON NEXT PAGE

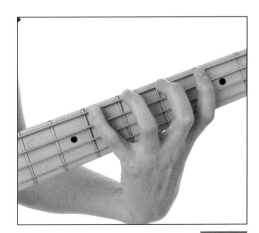

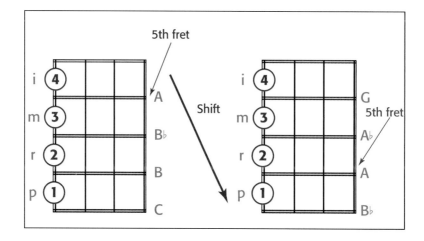

Finally, take a look at a more dramatic shift down the neck. You perform the same kind of hand motion you did earlier in the chapter, moving your entire fretting hand in one smooth motion. Start in the same position as in the previous exercises.

1. Play the C through A notes on the E string using the one-finger-per-fret method.

2. After playing the A note, smoothly move your hand in one motion down the neck so that the pinky finger lands on the 4th fret of the E string, or A flat (see photo).

3. Play the notes using the one-finger-per-fret method down to your index finger.

4. Lift your fingers from the fretboard, but keep your hand on the neck.

5. Play the open E string.

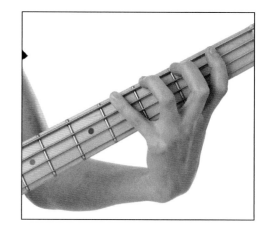

The notes you're playing with your middle and index fingers are G flat and F, respectively. The exercises here come to an end because you can't go any lower than the open E string. However, you can try starting with your pinky higher up the neck and shifting down from there. Get comfortable playing in all places on the neck.

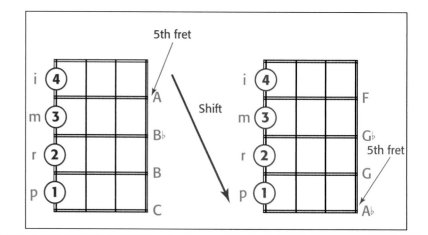

So far, all of the examples you've looked at take place on the *E* string. However, your bass has at least three more strings on it, so it might be a good idea to play on those as well. The exercises from earlier in this chapter are easily moved to the other strings, so this shouldn't feel much different. Your only concern at this point should be making sure that you fret each note on each string cleanly. Keep your other fingers close to the fingerboard, but out of the way of the note being fretted.

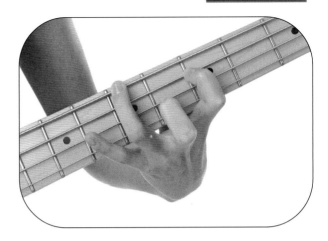

Shift-Across Exercises

Let's start with the first exercise from this chapter and move it to the other strings on the bass guitar.

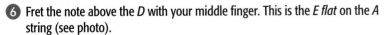

1. Fret the *A* on the *E* string with your index finger.

2. Play the *A* through *C* notes on the *E* string using the one-finger-per-fret technique.

3. As you play the *C* note on the *E* string, place your index finger just behind the 5th fret on the *A* string. Your wrist should flex just a little as you move from string to string, but it should stay straight overall.

4. Fret the note with your index finger. This note is called the *D* on the *A* string (see photo).

5. Play the *D* on the *A* string.

6. Fret the note above the *D* with your middle finger. This is the *E flat* on the *A* string (see photo).

7. Play the *E flat* on the *A* string.

CONTINUED ON NEXT PAGE

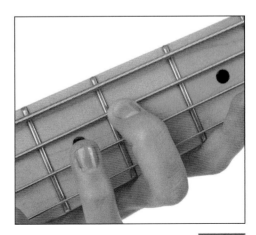

8 Fret the note above the *E flat* with your ring finger. This is the *E* on the *A* string (see photo).

9 Play the *E* on the *A* string.

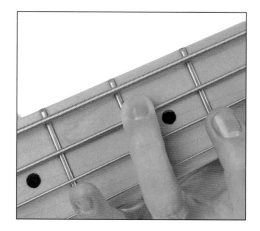

10 Fret the note above the *E* with your pinky finger (see photo). This is the *F* on the *A* string.

11 Play the *F* on the *A* string.

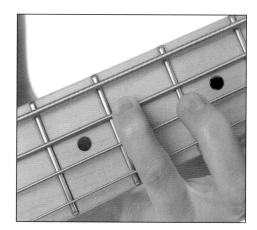

Notice how you're able to play all of these notes without having to shift your left hand at all. Your wrist moves slightly, using your thumb as a pivot point. However, aside from moving the fingers themselves over to the next string, you really didn't have to move your left hand at all. This lack of movement again helps to give you a consistent and even tone.

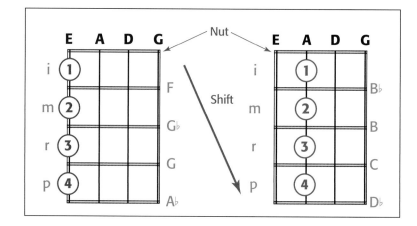

Try that same shift coming back down. Start with your pinky finger where you left off—fretting the *F* on the *A* string.

1 Starting with the pinky finger, play notes *F* through *D* on the *A* string going down using the one-finger-per-fret technique.

2 As you play the *D* on the *A* string, move your pinky above the *C* on the *E* string.

3 Fret the *C* on the *E* string with your pinky finger and play the note.

4 Play the *C* through *A* notes on the *E* string using the one-finger-per-fret method.

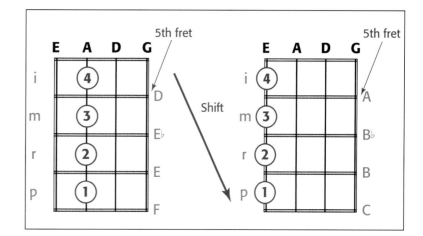

That takes care of moving across the *E* and *A* strings, but you don't have to stop there. Take these exercises and keep going up the fretboard, flexing your wrist just slightly each time to move to the next string up.

1 Starting with your index finger on the *A* on the *E* string, play *A* through *C* on the *E* string and *D* through *F* on the *A* string from the preceding example.

2 As you play the *F* on the *A* string, move your index finger over the 5th fret on the *D* string. This note is the *G* on the *D* string (see photo).

CONTINUED ON NEXT PAGE

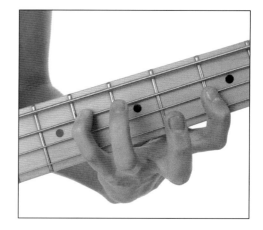

3 Play the *G* on the *D* string.

4 Fret the note above the *G* with your middle finger. This is the *A flat* on the *D* string (see photo).

5 Play the *A flat* on the *D* string.

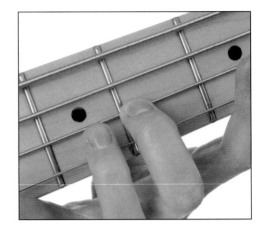

6 Fret the note above the *A flat* with your ring finger. This is the *A* on the *D* string (see photo).

7 Play the *A* on the *D* string.

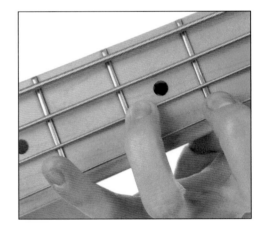

8 Fret the note above the *A* with your pinky finger. This is the *B flat* on the *D* string (see photo).

9 Play the *B flat* on the *D* string.

10 Continue the same motion up to the *G* string. The fret numbers are the same, but you are playing the notes *C, D flat, D,* and *E flat* on the *G* string (see diagram on the next page).

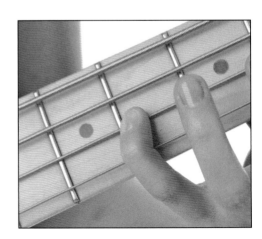

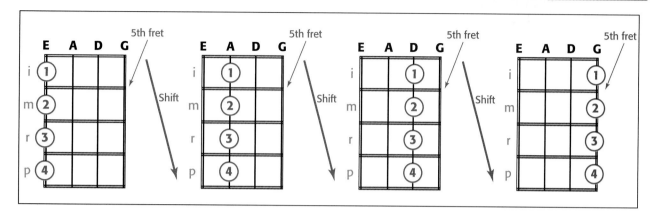

Now that you have these basic motions together, it's easy to apply them all over the fretboard. You should be able to start at any part of the fretboard on any finger and move from string to string or position to position with a minimum of shifting. Use the exercises from different points in this chapter and move them around the neck until you're comfortable playing in several different combinations at various parts of the fretboard. Concentrate for now on getting clear and ringing notes with your fingertips. You start working on getting the notes into a rhythm in Chapter 6.

Stay Close to the Fingerboard

You might have noticed throughout the exercises in this chapter that you don't move your fingers much until it's time to fret the next note. This economy of motion helps you move quickly from note to note without making your fingers do too much work.

Save Your Energy!

Imagine having to drive to the grocery store each time you wanted to buy a single item. You'll get everything you need, but you'll waste a lot of time and effort in the process. Doing what you need in a single trip means you get what you need done and you have the time and energy to do more.

Fingers too far from the neck

If you lift your fingers too far away from the strings after you're done with a note , that's all the more distance you'll have to bring them back when it's time to play the next note. The goal is to keep them as close as possible without interfering with the sounding of the notes.

Keeping your fingers with a slight curve close to the strings means you'll be ready to play the next note as soon as it needs to be played. Not only does it eventually increase your speed as a player, but it also keeps your hands from getting too tired too quickly. This kind of fine-motor movement can easily tire muscles unused to playing. Giving yourself more practice time to learn the fingerings (and develop calluses) helps you play better faster.

Fingers in proper fingerboard position

Finally, be prepared to spend some time with these exercises. With all the possible combinations of these exercises (such as playing the notes across the strings, and then shifting up and playing them back down or playing different fingerings all the way up a single string), there's a lot to do here. Take your time and explore. Your playing will be better for it. Conversely, rushing through these fundamentals will mean problems later down the road. Lay a good foundation to build your playing on. Gaps could mean bad habits, and bad habits will hinder your playing.

chapter 6

Plucking and Picking

So far, your left hand has been doing most of the work. But your right hand is just as important to playing the bass guitar. Whereas the left hand determines what note is played, the right hand dictates the volume and tone of that note. Using proper right-hand technique, you can make your bass guitar whisper or scream. This chapter shows you how to play the notes you want to hear.

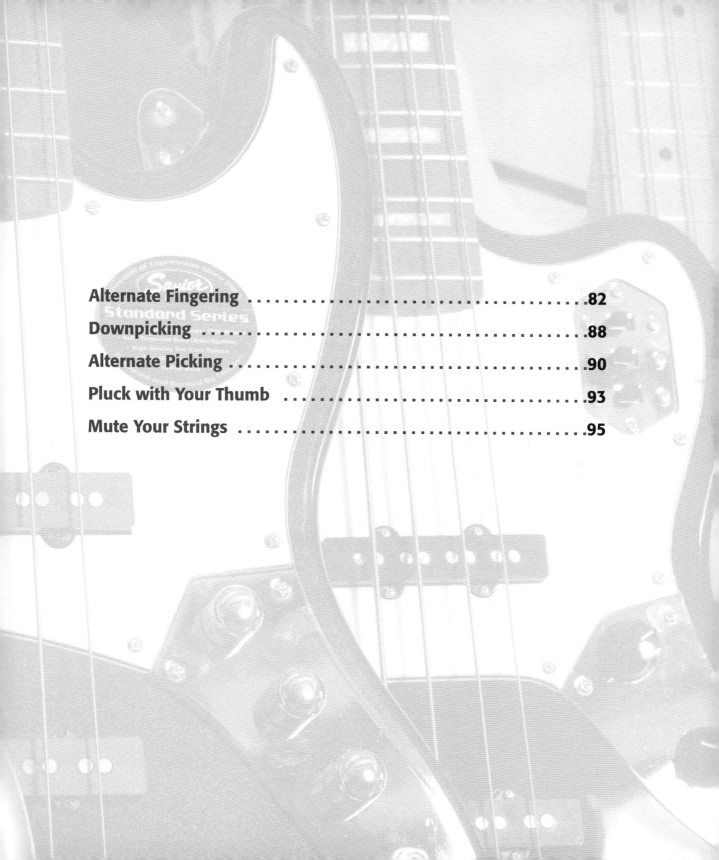

Alternate Fingering

Alternate fingering is perhaps the most common and versatile way to play the bass guitar. It's favored by many players because it allows you to build a strong, even sound while maintaining the ability to play fast. It also gives you a great degree of control over how the notes you play sound, from soft and smooth to loud and brash.

Left, Right, Left!

The key word for this playing style is *alternate.* You alternate playing the notes between the index and middle fingers of your right hand. After one finger plays a note, the other is right there, ready to play the following note. This alternation means you're ready to go with another note in any situation. The most important part to remember is that you alternate the fingers at all times. Your left finger always follows your right finger, and vice versa. This might seem a little strange at first, especially when you're crossing from one string to the next.

But practice this routine faithfully and you'll notice the benefits.

TIP

Shop around
You are introduced to several styles in this chapter. Although you'll probably settle on one as your favorite eventually, get to know all of them, no matter how difficult they seem at the beginning. Knowing the basics of each makes you a better and more versatile player.

Get the Feeling Down

The first step toward mastering alternate fingering is simple:

1 Fret the *A* on the *E* string, as you practiced in Chapter 5.

2 Pluck the note with your index finger by placing the pad of the finger underneath the *E* string and pulling up (see photo). Do this softly at first; you want enough force to make a note, but you don't want to pull the string too hard and cause it to snap back against the bass guitar.

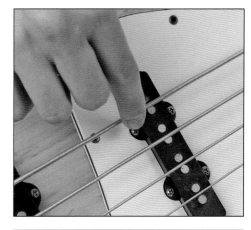

3 Pluck again with your middle finger (see photo), using the same amount of effort you used with your index finger.

At the beginning, repeating steps 2 and 3 should take up a great deal of your practice time. It might seem a little dull and repetitive at first, but the goal here is to become comfortable and familiar with alternating your fingers. Concentrate on making sure that you're always going from left to right and not throwing in groups or clusters of each finger. Just as with your left hand, it's important to make sure that your fingers move independently of each other and that you have the same amount of strength in each note.

TIP

Practice alternating fingers starting on either the index or middle finger as well. That way, no matter where you are while playing, you'll be able to keep that alternating pattern going.

CONTINUED ON NEXT PAGE

Move from String to String

Now that you've got the hang of alternate plucking on one string, try moving from string to string while keeping that alternation going. This takes some practice at first, but it's important to watch your fingers and force them to alternate.

Start this exercise by playing open notes on the *E* string. This time, the exercise concentrates solely on the right hand.

① Play four notes on the open *E* string, starting with your index finger. The sequence should go *index finger, middle finger, index finger, middle finger.*

② Now play four notes on the *A* string, using the same sequence.

③ Play four open notes on the *D* string in the same manner.

④ Finish up with four notes on the *G* string, just as you did on the other strings.

It's easy to maintain the alternating pattern in this exercise, because you're giving yourself enough time to see the shift to the next string coming and it's an even number of notes. That way, you always start the sequence on the index finger. Try this exercise again, but begin it on the middle finger this time around. This exercise uses the same notes, but it gets you used to leading with your middle finger as well.

In this next exercise, cut the number of notes in half:

 Play two notes on the open *E* string, starting with your index finger.

2 Now play two open notes on the *A* string.

3 Repeat this exercise for the *D* and *G* strings as well.

Again, you're starting each string with the same finger, but with fewer notes, to anticipate the shift. Again, repeat this exercise by starting on the middle finger. You should also repeat the previous two exercises starting on the *G* string and working your way down to the *E* string. Get comfortable moving in either direction.

Now that you're good at moving up and down the strings of the bass guitar with even amounts of notes, try playing an odd amount of notes on each string (see sequence on next page). This forces you to start each string on a different finger. It gets you ready to move from string to string more easily and quickly. This exercise is a little more challenging because you're leading with a different finger every time. Repeatedly practice this so that you're comfortable with that change. With a little time, you'll notice that it will become a natural movement. Again, repeat this exercise starting on the middle finger.

TIP

Repetition is key!
The best way to make these motions feel natural is regular practice. Start slow and keep at it. It's important to make this a natural part of your playing.

CONTINUED ON NEXT PAGE

1 Play three notes on the open *E* string, beginning on your index finger. The sequence should go *index finger, middle finger, index finger.*

2 Now play three open notes on the *A* string, beginning with your middle finger. Now, you'll play those notes with a sequence of *middle finger, index finger, middle finger.*

3 Play three open notes on the *D* string, starting with your index finger. This is the same sequence as the *E* string.

4 End up by playing three open notes on the *G* string, using the same sequence as the *A* string. If you do this exercise correctly, you end up playing the last note with your middle finger.

Finally, throw out all the extra notes and practice playing each open string with a different plucking finger.

1 Pluck an open *E* note with your index finger.

2 Pluck an open *A* note with your middle finger.

3 Pluck an open *D* note with your index finger.

4 Pluck an open *G* note with your middle finger.

Just like the rest, repeat the previous two exercises starting on your middle finger and starting on the *G* string instead of the *E* string. In fact, you should probably go back and repeat all the exercises in this section again. And again. Repetition might seem a little boring right now, but it's the key to building a strong, even alternate picking style. Your goal is to make sure that each note gets the same tone and emphasis as the rest of the notes you play, no matter whether you're playing softly or roaring loudly. Your goal is consistency.

Once you feel comfortable with all of these exercises, you can mix up which notes you play on each string as you move up, as long as you concentrate on alternating your index and middle fingers. The songs you play might not have even groups of notes on each string, so it's important to get used to switching off.

TIP

Switch it up!
It's easy to get into a safe and comfortable routine with these kinds of exercises. Make sure you switch up your routines every so often to expand your playing abilities. Never be afraid to try something different.

Downpicking

Although the alternate plucking technique is a favorite of many bassists, many have also borrowed a trick from guitarists and use a pick. Chapter 3 reviewed how to hold a pick, so refer back to that section for a refresher if you need to. Now, look at how to play using the downpicking technique.

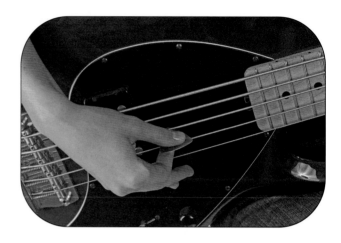

Take It Down

Just as the name of the technique implies, you use the pick only in a downward motion; that is, you move the pick down, striking the string from the top. As opposed to strumming a guitar, however, you'll want to play only one note at a time right now. After each stroke, bring the pick back above the string and get ready for the next downstroke.

Don't bend your wrist as in the photo; instead let your elbow do the work. Try to keep your wrist as straight as possible and use your elbow to power your downstrokes. You'll have to use just a slight amount of movement to accomplish the downstroke, and it puts less strain on your wrist as you play.

Now repeat this downstroke while fretting the *A* note on the *E* string for a few minutes. Concentrate on making even, strong notes on each stroke. Most players use downpicking to create aggressive, pumping bass lines in hard-rock and metal styles. Using only downstrokes gives each note a lot of power and definition, making it suitable for those types of music.

Apply some of the exercises from earlier in this chapter to downpicking now:

1 Pick four notes on the open *E* string. Concentrate on making each one even and strong.

2 Pick four notes on the open *A* string.

3 Pick four notes on the open *D* string.

4 Pick four notes on the open *G* string.

You don't have to worry about how you start playing each string in this case because every stroke is a downstroke. It is a good idea to start this exercise on the *G* string as well as the *E* string, however. Even though you're always using downstrokes with this technique, you should get used to moving from string to string in either direction. Practice the previous exercises using three notes, two notes, and one note as well.

Down to Earth

It's important not to get too carried away with your downstrokes and strike other strings as you play. You need just a slight movement of your elbow (as shown in the photos) to make the pick strike the strings correctly. Overdoing it causes a great deal of unwanted noise. To help accomplish this, a lot of players use *palm muting,* a technique you look at later in this chapter. Until then, however, focus on using just enough effort to get a clear note without making any other noise.

Now that you've looked at picking using just downstrokes, move on to using upstrokes as well.

Alternate Picking

This style of picking adds an upstroke—or striking the string from the bottom up—to the down-stroke you already learned. As you might suspect, this style allows you to add a little more speed to your playing, as you'll take the motion you'd normally use to raise the pick for another downstroke to play another note. The key here is to make that motion sound as much like the downstroke as possible.

Alternate Picking Exercises

Start by fretting the *A* note on the *E* string, and pick that note using a downstroke. Just as you normally would, stop the pick before it hits the next string. This time, however, strike the string with the pick on the way back up. You should use the same amount of effort as you do with the downstroke; you're just using the same motion in reverse.

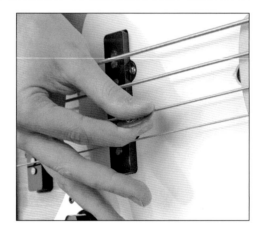

Run through some familiar exercises now using alternate picking. Instead of specifying index or middle fingers, however, use up- and downstrokes:

1 Play four notes on the open *E* string. The sequence should be *down, up, down, up.*

2 Play four notes on the open *A* string, using the same sequence.

3 Repeat the exercise on the *D* (see photo) and *G* strings.

When moving between strings, just move your arm a little bit to the next string. It should be an easy, fluid motion. Just make sure you don't accidentally hit another string in that motion. Try the same exercise now, using just two notes per string.

1 Play two notes on the open *E* string. The sequence should be *down, up, down, up.*

2 Play two notes on the open *A* string, using the same sequence.

3 Repeat the exercise on the *D* and *G* strings.

You're switching strings a little more quickly this time; however, the basics remain the same. Repeat these exercises beginning on upstrokes now, and try them beginning on the *G* string as well. You might find it easier to start with an upstroke on the *G* string, but be sure to practice it beginning on a downstroke as well.

On the following page, you will take a look at odd groups of notes now. This gets a little more complicated because you switch strings and use upstrokes at the same time. Practice these slowly and remember to move your entire forearm in one smooth motion.

1 Play three notes on the open *E* string, beginning with a downstroke. The sequence should go *down, up, down.*

2 Now play three open notes on the *A* string, beginning with an upstroke. Now, play those notes with a sequence of *up, down, up.*

3 Play three open notes on the *D* string, starting with a downstroke. This is the same sequence as you played on the *E* string.

4 End up by playing three open notes on the *G* string, using the same sequence as on the *A* string. If you do this exercise correctly, you end up playing the last note with an upstroke.

CONTINUED ON NEXT PAGE

Practice this until it becomes a smooth motion. Then move on to playing just one note per string. Again, use just slight motions of your arm to keep things from flying out of control.

1 Play an open *E* note with a downstroke.

2 Pluck an open *A* note with an upstroke.

3 Pluck an open *D* note with a downstroke.

4 Pluck an open *G* note with an upstroke.

Again, this takes some concentration to make sure you hit these notes correctly without causing excess string noise or ringing. That's why it's key to use smooth, precise motions without swinging too wildly. There will be times for swinging wildly at notes, but those usually come at the end of the encore. Pace yourself until then.

Plucking notes with the thumb is an older style of playing taken from the fingerpicking style of guitar playing. In that style, the thumb is reserved for playing bass notes, so it only makes sense that it would work its way over to the bass guitar. However, this isn't a commonly used technique because it doesn't lend itself to quick or easy playing. It's used mainly when you want a deep and dense sound, such as a country, folk, or slower jazz feel.

Please be aware that this is not the same technique as slapping the bass, which is often referred to as *thumbstyle* bass. That technique is covered in Chapter 11.

Hand Position for Thumb Plucking

There are two ways to position your right hand for this style of playing. One way is to place the tips of your fingers below the *G* string and rest your thumb on the strings themselves.

You can also rest the edge of your palm on the bridge of the bass guitar (not on the strings, but on the actual metal of the bridge) and again rest your thumb on the strings of the bass guitar.

This technique uses downstrokes of the thumb to play the notes. Again, this isn't meant to produce quick successions of notes, but instead to produce deep, dense notes, similar to the sound of an upright bass.

CONTINUED ON NEXT PAGE

Fret the *D* note on the *A* string with your left hand. Play that note with your thumb, plucking down on the string.

You can either let the note ring out or just bring your thumb back to rest on that string, stopping the sound of the note. This is especially useful for music that requires space between the notes, such as country and folk.

Now take the exercises from earlier in this section and apply them to your thumb:

1 Pick four notes on the open *E* string. Concentrate on making each one even and strong.

2 Pick four notes on the open *A* string.

3 Pick four notes on the open *D* string.

4 Pick four notes on the open *G* string.

Now, do the same exercise, but bring your thumb back up to rest on the string in place of some of the notes.

1 Pick two notes on the open *E* string. Bring your thumb back up to rest on the string between notes.

2 Pick two notes on the open *A* string. Bring your thumb back up to rest on the string between notes.

3 Repeat this exercise on the *D* and *G* strings.

This style of playing lends itself naturally to country and the "two-feel" style of jazz, which makes extensive use of space between each note. If you've ever been to a formal dance or a wedding, you've heard this type of music. You probably won't use your thumb too much if you're playing fast pop or rock; however, it's a useful tool to have available. It's also a good technique to use with palm muting to produce a low "thump" suited for country music. For more on palm muting, see the next page.

So far, this chapter has dealt with creating notes with different types of plucking and picking. You might have noticed as you play that sometimes other strings sound along with the notes you meant to play, or that strings continue to sound after you've finished with the note you meant to play. The first case of unwanted ringing is caused by *sympathetic vibration*. The motion of one string causes vibrations in the other strings as well, and the pickup translates that motion into sound. The second case is just the after-effects of playing a note—once you play it, it's going to ring for a little bit.

Hit the Mute Button

The answer to both of these unwanted noise problems is string muting. Simply put, resting your fingers on strings causes them to stop vibrating. You can either use your left hand to stop the vibrations on the neck, or you can use your right hand to stop or alter the vibrations closer to the bridge. Each is a valuable technique to learn, and each has its own musical applications as well.

CONTINUED ON NEXT PAGE

THE LEFT HAND

Left-handed muting is based on techniques you learned in Chapter 5. Remember that the emphasis in that chapter was on fretting the note directly behind the fret and keeping your fingers close to the fingerboard.

The easiest way to mute a note with your left hand is to simply lift your finger enough to bring the string off of the fretboard. Your finger should remain on the string, however. Doing this prevents any further string vibrations, effectively stopping the note. This is useful when you want to play a quick series of notes with definite space in between each note.

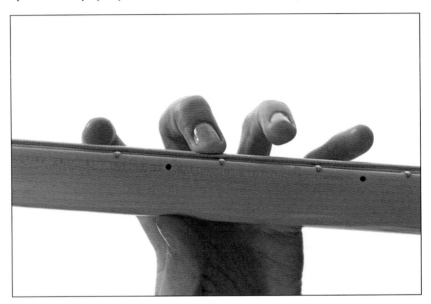

In this exercise, fret the *A* note on the *E* string:

1. Using the alternate plucking technique, play four *A* notes.
2. Now play the same four notes again, but pick up your finger between each note.
3. Fret the *D* note on the *A* string.
4. Play four *D* notes, picking up your finger between each note.
5. Fret the *G* note on the *D* string.
6. Play four *G* notes, picking up your finger between each note.
7. Fret the *C* note on the *G* string.
8. Play four *C* notes, picking up your finger between each note.

Notice how each time you pick up your finger, the note stops. This works well for stopping the notes you just played, but it doesn't do much to stop the sympathetic vibrations of the other strings. In this case, use your other fingers to stop the other strings from ringing.

USE YOUR FINGERS

When you aren't using the fingers on your left hand to fret notes, you can use them to stop other strings from ringing. Simply rest them gently across the strings over the fretboard. Be careful not to actually fret a note with the other fingers. You want to put just enough pressure on them to keep them from ringing.

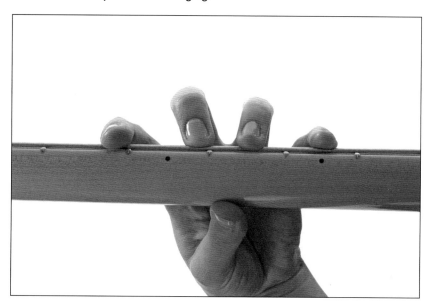

In this exercise, fret the *A* note on the *E* string with your index finger and let the other fingers on your left hand rest gently on the other strings. Make sure that you don't let the other fingers rest on the *E* string; that prevents the note you want to play from sounding out correctly.

1 Play four *A* notes with your left hand muting the strings.

2 Lift the fingers on your left hand except for the index finger.

3 Play the notes again. Note the sympathetic vibrations from the other strings.

4 Bring your fingers down on the strings lightly to stop the vibrations.

5 Play the four *A* notes again.

You can repeat this exercise on the other strings as well. When you're playing a lot of notes on one string, as in the exercises in Chapter 5, you can lightly rest the edge of your palm on the strings to stop the string vibrations. Again, be sure to stay out of the way of the notes you actually intend to play. Your ultimate goal is the ability to start and stop notes exactly when you want to. With practice, this comes naturally.

CONTINUED ON NEXT PAGE

THE RIGHT HAND

Your other choice for muting notes involves your right hand. You can use your right hand to either stop notes or give them a chunkier, thicker sound.

First, look at a good right-hand muting style using the alternate plucking technique. When you're plucking the strings, let the finger that just plucked the note come to rest briefly on the next string up (notice index finger in photo below). For example, if you're playing a note on the *A* string, let the plucking finger come to rest on the *E* string. Try this exercise:

1 Fret the *D* note on the *A* string.

2 Play this note four times, letting the plucking finger come to rest on the *E* string.

3 Fret the *G* note on the *D* string.

4 Play this note four times, letting the plucking finger come to rest on the *A* string.

5 Fret the *C* note on the *G* string.

6 Play this note four times, letting the plucking finger come to rest on the *D* string.

Obviously, this technique doesn't work on the *E* string because there's nothing to rest on after you play a note. You can use the other plucking finger to stop the vibrations of the strings, as long as it works into the alternation of your picking style. Otherwise, you might consider using more left-handed muting in addition to this style to prevent sympathetic vibrations. Both hands should work in tandem to make sure that the only notes you hear are the ones you want to hear.

PALM MUTING

Another right-handed muting option involves resting the edge of your palm against the strings just above the bridge saddles. You can still hear the notes you play, but the other strings don't vibrate at all. The notes you do hear are short and thick. This technique is used a great deal in rock and metal, usually in quieter, driving passages.

This muting style works best when you're plucking with your thumb or using a pick. Use both techniques when playing the exercises in this section.

1 Rest the edge of your right palm against the strings just above the saddles on the bridge of your bass guitar.

2 Play four notes on the open *E* string. Notice the added "thump" to the sound and the speed at which the notes stop.

3 Repeat this on the other open strings.

4 Now fret the *A* on the *E* string and play four notes on that string.

5 Repeat using the other strings fretted at the 5th fret.

You can also use this muting technique on the exercises in Chapter 5. Notice the difference in sounds between when you first played the exercises and the sound you get now with palm muting. This probably isn't a technique you'll use for all of your playing, but it is a nice ability to have available when the need arises.

Make It All Work Together

You'll probably want to use a combination of left- and right-handed muting techniques as you play. Some you'll use to stop unwanted sounds, and some you'll use to alter the tone of the notes you're playing. There are no hard-and-fast rules on what technique to use where. It all depends on the song you're playing.

Practice each technique until you're comfortable using it, and let your ears tell you which one sounds the best in each situation. This is an instinct you can develop only over time. Listen to lots of music and pay attention to the bass guitar sound. By hearing different examples, you get a better sense of what goes where.

chapter 7

Playing Your First Scales

Now that you've got your technique together, take a look at the building blocks of every bass line. Learning scales and how to read both standard notation and tablature lets you learn real music that much more quickly. This is where you take the notes you've played and make them make sense. In this chapter, you pick up the basics for material that's used in the rest of the book.

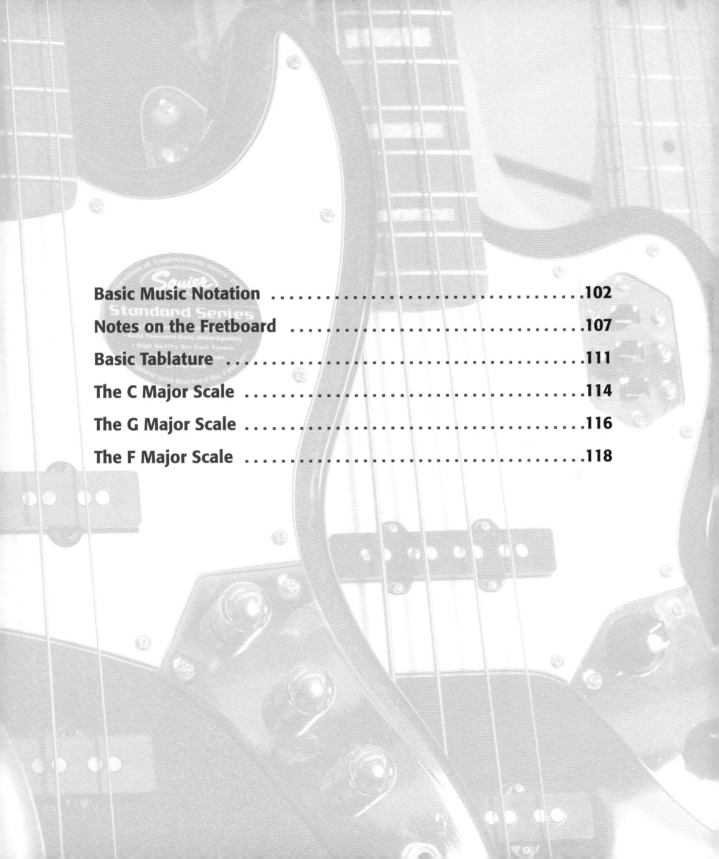

Basic Music Notation

Whether you're new to sheet music or you just need a refresher course, it's good to take some time and learn how to read music. We're not going to get into reading Bach cantatas or anything, but it will come in handy down the road to be able to read some basic scales and rhythms.

The Bass Clef and Key/Time Signatures

The notes on the bass guitar fall squarely into the appropriately named *bass clef.* Following the bass clef symbol is the *key signature*, a combination of symbols that tells you the key the song is in. It also sometimes tells you what notes the lines and spaces on the staff represent.

The *key* identifies one central note and the rest of the notes in a particular scale. We'll get to scales later in this chapter. For now, just keep in mind that the symbols following the bass clef represent sharp and flat notes.

Bass clef symbol

Making a note *sharp* means raising it one half-step above the normal note. In terms of a bass guitar, that's one fret higher. A *flat* note is one half-step below the normal note, or one fret lower. The symbols after the bass clef show you which notes are flat, normal, or sharp throughout the whole piece of music.

Bass clef with sharp symbol

Bass clef with flat symbol

The *natural* symbol returns the note to its unflattened or unsharpened state. For instance if A♭ existed in the key signature (meaning every A in the piece of music is automatically flattened), and there was a natural sign in front of one specific A in the piece, then only for that 'naturalized' A you would play a regular A, then go back to flattening every other A. These symbols (flats, sharps, and naturals) that pop up here and there later on in the music are collectively called *accidentals*.

Natural symbol

After the clef and the flats or sharps (if any) comes the *time signature.* This looks like two numbers stacked on top of each other. The top number tells how many beats there are to a *measure,* or unit of written music. The bottom number tells you what type of note receives that beat. See the next two sections for more on the different types of notes and what I mean when I say "receives the beat."

4/4 time signature

All of these parts put together look like the figure shown here. This particular design is for the G Major key.

CONTINUED ON NEXT PAGE

G Major key signature

TIP

Everything Is natural
All notes are natural unless otherwise specified in the key signature or an accidental. You'll never see a natural symbol in the key signature.

Basic Music Notation *(continued)*

The Notes

Now take a look at the notes themselves. Each note identifies how many beats it receives in a measure.

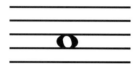

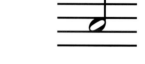

A whole note *receives (is 'held' for) four beats per measure.*

The half note *receives two beats per measure.*

The quarter note *receives one beat per measure.*

The eighth note *receives half the beat value of the quarter note.*

Finally, the sixteenth note *receives half the beat value of the eighth note.*

Use this figure to keep all the beat values straight.

1 whole note =   2 half notes   =   4 quarter notes   =   8 eighth notes

= 16 sixteenth notes

The Staff

All of the notes are placed on the *staff*, which is made up of five lines stretching across the page.

Just as you can tell the beat value of a note by its shape, you can tell the pitch of a note by where it's placed on the staff. Look at one of the exercises from Chapter 6, where you played four notes on each open string using the alternate fingering technique. Remember that the strings on the bass guitar are *E, A, D,* and *G,* from lowest to highest.

If a note appears below or above the main staff, like the open *E* string (shown below), it is printed on its own smaller line. This is called a *ledger* (also sometimes spelled *leger*) *line.*

Notice the lines (called barlines) between each group of four notes. Each line marks off a *measure* (or *bar*) of music. Each measure contains the number of beats set aside in the time signature. If the time signature is 4/4, there are 4 beats per measure. If it's 3/4, there are three beats.

See how easy that is? You're already reading music! Let's take a look at the rest of the notes on the staff.

Letter names of staff lines

Letter names of staff spaces

Grade-school teachers use mnemonic devices to teach the order of letters on the staff. You can use "Good Boys Do Fine Always" to remember the order of the lines and "All Cats Expect Greatness" for the spaces, or you can make up something else entirely. The musical alphabet runs from *A* to *G.* Notice how the staff lines and spaces follow this order.

CONTINUED ON NEXT PAGE

Basic Music Notation *(continued)*

Rests

Knowing when not to play is just as important as knowing what to play. *Rests* indicate where (and for how long) you don't play anything. Just like the notes, there are markings for whole, half, quarter, sixteenth, and thirty-second rests.

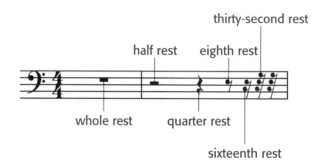

You'll play again the *E, A, D, G* open string exercise you saw in Chapter 6, but this time substitute a quarter rest for the third note in each group. It looks like this:

Instead of playing the third note in this exercise, don't play anything. While you play, count to yourself "1-2-3-4," and don't play anything when you say "3." You can use string muting here, as described in Chapter 6.

The preceding chapters have shown you some of the notes on the bass guitar fretboard. You should know by now that the open strings are *E, A, D,* and *G,* from lowest to highest. You should also know that the fifth fret of each string is the same note as the next open string. Take a look at the rest of the notes on the fretboard now.

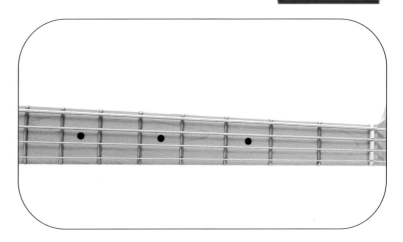

Mapping Out the Notes

Don't be intimidated by all of the notes you see. There are really only 12 notes on the bass guitar—they just repeat at lower or higher frequencies (or *octaves*). Once you've learned the pattern and notice a few landmarks, it'll be easy to remember.

First, learn the 12 notes on the bass guitar. These notes are the same as those played on many other instruments, from the piano to the saxophone. If you know the alphabet, you know these notes.

A A#/B♭ B C C#/D♭ D D#/E♭ E F F#/G♭ G G#/A♭

The notes separated by slashes are actually the same note. Those notes just go by different names depending on what key you're playing at the time. They're called *enharmonic equivalents,* but you don't need to remember that right now. Just remember that the same note can have two separate names.

You're familiar with the fretboard by now, so you should be able to match up the note names listed on the diagram on the next page to your own bass guitar.

CONTINUED ON NEXT PAGE

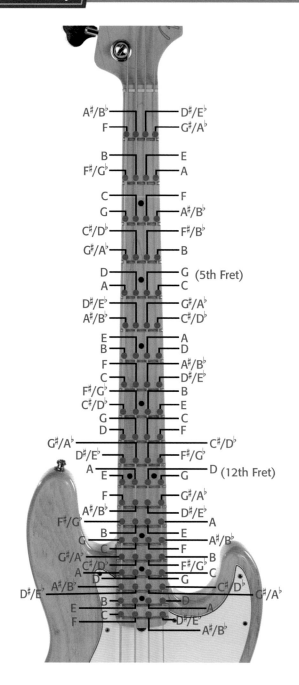

If you look closely, you should notice a pattern in how these notes are laid out across the fingerboard. Most bass guitars also have helpful hints directly on the fingerboard. For example, most have dots or some other sort of inlaid material on the 3rd, the 5th, the 7th, the 9th, the 12th, the 15th, the 17th, and the 19th frets. The pattern continues if a certain bass guitar has more frets.

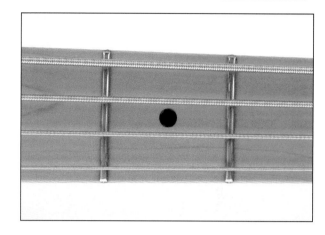

These are just handy placeholders that remind you where you are and help you find your position quickly. Many bass guitars also have similar dots on the side of the neck for easier viewing while playing.

It's a good idea to use these as quick visual indicators, but don't grow too reliant on staring at the fretboard while you're playing. Eventually, you'll want your ears to do the work of telling you where you are and what you're playing. Still, it's great to have these reminders there when you have to quickly orient yourself on the fretboard.

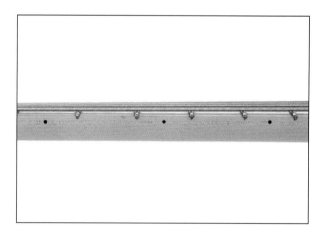

The inlays on the 12th fret are often different from the others on the fretboard. They might range from double dots to an intricate design, depending on who made the instrument. The reason for this special design is that the 12th fret represents a significant change in the layout of the notes. Playing a note on the 12th fret means you're playing the exact same note as the open string that note is on, only an *octave* up. In the major and minor scales there are eight notes. Although the notes get higher in pitch, they still have the same names. Each group is just in a higher or lower octave.

CONTINUED ON NEXT PAGE

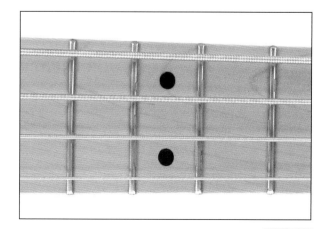

The upshot of all this is that the notes above the 12th fret are in the same order as the ones between the nut and the 12th fret. Once you've got the lower part of the fretboard memorized, you can repeat those note names for all the frets above the 12th fret as well.

The next group of exercises focuses on taking the notes and fingerings you've already played and attaching them to the note names you just learned. The easiest way to do this is to play the exercises slowly and say the note names to yourself as you go.

① Play the open *E* string and say "E."

② Fret the 4th fret on the *E* string with your index finger and say "A♭."

③ Fret the 5th fret with your middle finger and say "A."

④ Fret the 6th fret with your ring finger and say "B♭."

⑤ Fret the 7th fret with your pinky and say "B."

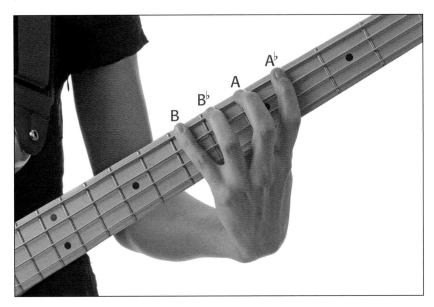

Repeat the exercises you've learned so far, saying the notes as you play them. Start slowly and refer to the diagram of the fretboard as you go. Practicing this helps you learn the fingerboard and reinforces the note names as you go.

Basic Tablature

If standard music notation is the *War and Peace* of sheet music, *tablature* is the CliffsNotes. Tablature won't tell you the entire story, but it will help you find your way through the music and learn possible fingerings for notes. It's also a good way to pass along information to other people.

How to Read Tablature

Tablature looks similar to the bass clef staff, but there are only four lines in this case. As you can see by the note names below, these lines represent the strings on the bass guitar. To represent fingerings, numbers are placed on those lines. These represent the frets to be played while following the tablature. You won't see any note names, but you will see where to put your fingers.

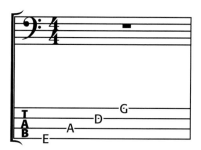

CONTINUED ON NEXT PAGE

This is the tablature, or *tab* for short, for the exercise used earlier in this chapter. It's helpful because you can see exactly where to put your fingers, but it doesn't give you all the information you need to play the exercise. Although you know where to put your fingers, you don't know how long to play those notes or where any rests might be. That's why tab is best used in conjunction with standard notation.

The notation shows you the notes and the rhythm, whereas the tablature shows you on which frets to play the exercise. The tablature isn't especially helpful here, but it will come in handy later. As you've seen from the earlier diagrams, there are several places on the fretboard to play the same note. The tablature shows you one way to play it, based on the experience of the music's author.

TIP

Check the 'Net

The Internet is a great source of additional information on the bass guitar. Check out bassplayer.com, talkbass.com, activebass.com, and theuglybassplayer.com for more information.

You can find a wealth of tab resources on the Internet that show you how to play your favorite songs. To use these tab examples, you need to be extremely familiar with the music you're playing. But the tab shows you recommended fingerings and can help you get the song ready.

The C Major Scale

All of the exercises you've looked at to this point were based on learning the fretboard of the bass guitar. However, most of the music you've heard on the radio isn't based on playing notes up and down the fretboard like that. The vast majority of Western music is based on *scales*, or groups of notes based around a central note, or *key*.

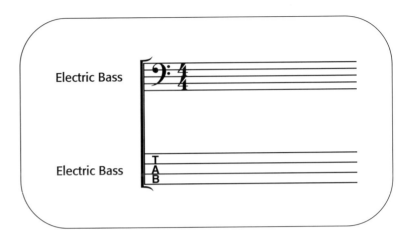

How to Play a C Major Scale

The most important scale to start with is the major scale. This typically sounds happy and bright to a listener's ear. And the best place to start with the major scale is C Major, because there aren't any sharps or flats to remember when you play it.

You can tell whether a piece of music is in C Major if there are no sharp or flat symbols after the bass clef (see the figure above). From there, it's a simple matter of counting off the alphabet beginning with *C* to get the notes in the C Major scale.

C   D   E   F   G   A   B   C

Take a look at how those notes are shown on the bass-clef staff. As you look at each note, say the note name to yourself, from the lower *C* note to the higher *C* note. There are a couple of ways to play this particular scale, and this is where tablature comes in handy.

The first sample fingering starts with your middle finger on the *C* on the *A* string. Your hand shouldn't move from its basic position. Be sure to use the one-finger-per-fret technique. In this case, the letter "m" stands for the middle finger, "p" stands for the pinky, "i" stands for the index finger, and "r" stands for the ring finger.

① Play each note on the frets listed in the tablature.

② Say the name of the note as you play it. It's always going to be the next letter in the alphabet.

③ Look at the letters above the notes. Those letters tell you which finger to play the note with.

Electric Bass

Electric Bass

```
m   p   i   m     p   i   r   p
                                2—4—5
                      2—3   5
          3—5
```

That same scale can be played with the same fingering at a different place on the neck. Look at this example and go through the same steps as in the first C Major scale example.

Electric Bass

Electric Bass

```
m   p   i   m     p   i   r   p
                                7—9—10
                      7—8   10
          8—10
```

Finally, look at another way to play this scale. This method involves stretching your hand a little more. Take this one slowly.

This fingering might seem a little unnatural at first, but it helps you look for different places to play the same note on the fretboard. This comes in handy later. Practice these fingerings repeatedly until it feels natural to play them.

Electric Bass

Electric Bass

```
    i   m   p   i     m   p   m   r
                                4—5
                        3   5—7
        3—5—7
```

The G Major Scale

The G Major scale is a close relative of the C Major scale. Most of the notes are common, except that there is one sharp note found in the G Major scale. You can recognize the G Major scale by seeing the one sharp symbol following the bass clef. That one sharp is placed on the line for the *F* note, meaning that note is sharp throughout the piece.

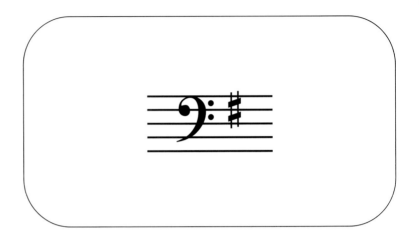

How to Play a G Major Scale

To learn the notes in the G Major scale, count off the letters in the alphabet beginning with *G*. Once you hit *A*, start the alphabet again and go until you hit *G*. When you get to *F*, say that note as "F sharp."

G   A   B   C   D   E   F#   G

Remember, that sharp means that the note is one half-step higher than the regular *F*, meaning that it's one fret higher.

You can use several of the same fingerings for the G Major scale as you did for the C Major scale. Look at the first example, starting with your middle finger on the *G* note on the *E* string. Again, your hand shouldn't move from its basic position. Be sure to use the one-finger-per-fret technique.

1 Play each note on the frets listed in the tablature.

2 Say the name of the note as you play it. It's always going to be the next letter in the alphabet.

3 Look at the letters above the note. Those letters tell you which finger to play the note with.

Because this *G* note is one of the lowest notes on the bass guitar neck, this is the only place you can use this fingering for the G Major scale in this octave. However, you could play this scale up an octave higher on the neck and still use the same fingering. Start this example at the 10th fret on the *A* string.

The "8va" above the notes just means to play that passage an octave up from where it is notated. In this example, the letters below the notes show you which fingers to use. The tablature shows you exactly where to play the notes.

Now go back to the lower *G* note on the *E* string and start on the index finger.

The F Major Scale

Like the G Major scale, the F Major scale shares many of the same notes as the C Major scale. In this case, however, there's a flat note instead of a sharp note to differentiate the scale. That flat is placed on the line for the B note, meaning that all B notes in that piece are flat.

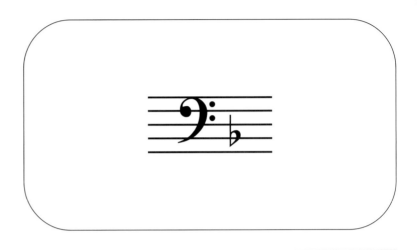

How to Play an F Major Scale

To learn the notes in the F Major scale, count off the letters in the alphabet beginning and ending with *F,* again going back to *A* after *G.* Remember to say "B flat" instead of "B."

F   G   A   B♭   C   D   E   F

Remember, that flat means that the note is one half-step lower than the regular *B,* meaning that it's one fret lower.

These fingerings should look familiar at this point. Start the first example on the lower *F* note on the *E* string. Again, your hand shouldn't move from its basic position. Be sure to use the one-finger-per-fret technique.

① Play each note on the frets listed in the tablature.

② Say the name of the note as you play it. It's always going to be the next letter in the alphabet.

③ Look at the letters underneath the note. Those letters tell you which finger to play the note with.

Now move this scale up an octave, but stay on the same string. Start this example at the 13th fret on the *A* string.

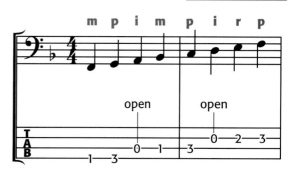

Return to the lower *F* note on the *E* string and start on the index finger.

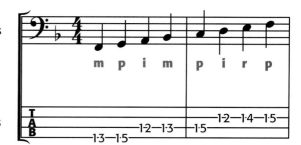

Listen to the difference between the first example of playing this scale using open strings and the third example using fretted notes. You're playing the same basic notes, but they have a little different *timbre* (pronounced *tamber*), or are different in tone and sound. Knowing what your instrument sounds like at different parts on the fretboard can help you determine how you want to play different scales and songs.

These scales not only help you learn the notes on the fretboard, but they should also sound a little familiar. Most of the songs you've heard have been based off of these types of scales, just in different keys. This should get you started and familiar with the concept of scales.

Playing with Chords

The bass guitar's job is to lay the foundation of the song being played. Because most Western music is based on chords, it's important for a bassist to know what makes a chord and how they fit into the song. In this chapter, you take scales and notes you already know and make them into chords.

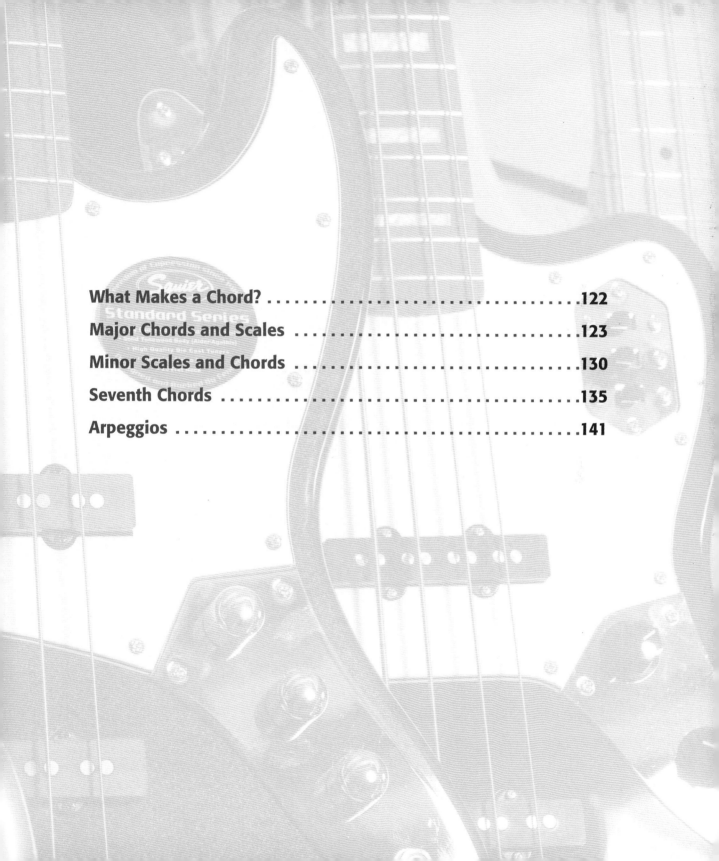

What Makes a Chord?

One of the basic building blocks of most of the music you listen to is harmony. In most modern music, harmony is represented by the playing of *chords*. Chords are groups or clusters of notes played within a certain time-frame. A chord could be played by one guitar or piano or a full orchestra, but it's still a chord.

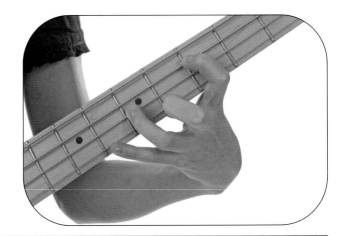

THE INGREDIENTS

Each chord has a fundamental note, or *root note*. That root defines the basis of the chord, and the name of the chord is usually derived from the root note. From there, the other notes played define the character and nature of the chord.

As a bassist, your job is often to set the root note of the chord. Most people hear the lowest pitch played as the root of the chord, while other instruments provide the color. However, it's not always that way. Bass lines can also be expected to provide many other notes beyond the root note to keep the music interesting.

That's why it's important to know how to build a chord and play all of the notes in it. You never know what's going to help make the song more interesting, so you have to be ready to provide any of the appropriate notes at any time to make everything flow smoothly.

CHORD SHORTHAND

Because the names of the exact notes in each chord can vary depending on the scale and type of chord, a common shorthand of describing the notes in a chord uses Roman numerals to take the place of those exact names.

I	ii	iii	IV	V	vi	vii	VIII

In this case, the *I* always refers to the root of the scale. So if you were looking at the C Major scale, the *I* would equal the *C.* The rest of the notes in the scale would fall into place from there.

C	D	E	F	G	A	B	C
I	ii	iii	IV	V	vi	vii	VIII

Aside from the root, each of the notes in the Roman numeral shorthand takes its name from its number. For example, the *V* note of each scale is called the *fifth,* the *vi* note is called the *sixth,* and so on. The *VIII* note is called the *octave* note.

These names are important to remember because chords actually take their names from the Roman numerals of the notes involved. Before we get to that, however, take a look at the basic major and minor chords. In both of these cases, the chords are made from the root, the third (*iii*), and the fifth (*V*) note of their respective scales. For these chords and the vast majority of the others you'll learn, these three notes are involved.

Just like the scales they come from, major chords often sound happier and more cheerful to the listener. They're also the easiest chords to build because you just take the root, third, and fifth of the scales to build them.

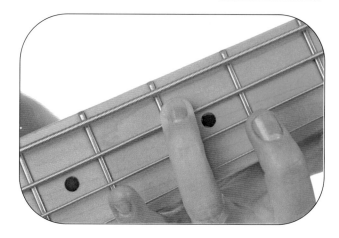

Construct a Major Chord

C MAJOR CHORD

Start with the C Major scale (see page 114). To make a C Major chord, (a) take the root—*C*—the third—*E*—and the fifth—*G*.

Now, find these notes on the bass guitar. Take a look at one way to play the notes in the C Major scale. Instead of playing all the notes in the scale, just play these three notes (b). Now take a look at an alternate fingering (c). Notice how these notes are related to the scales you played in the preceding chapter. With that in mind, check out this alternate fingering (d).

a

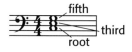

C Major chord

b

Middle finger on C: A string

c

Middle finger on C: E string

d

Index finger on C: A string

CONTINUED ON NEXT PAGE

G MAJOR CHORD

In the G Major scale, the chord notes are *G, B,* and *D.*

You can figure out the G Major chord fingerings from the scale work you did in Chapter 7 as well.

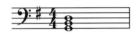

G Major chord

Middle finger on lower G: E string

Middle finger on G: A string (10th fret)

Index finger on lower G: E string

F MAJOR CHORD

In the F Major scale, the chord notes are *F, A,* and *C.*

Just like the other scales, take the root, third, and fifth notes from this scale in different fingerings and play the F Major chord from there.

F Major chord

Middle finger on lower F: E string

Middle finger on F: D string

Index finger on lower F: E string

Now, take a look at the other major scales and a sample fingering for their major chords. Start with the major scales that have sharps in them, such as the G Major scale, and then look at the scales with flats in them, such as the F Major scale.

CONTINUED ON NEXT PAGE

Major Chords and Scales *(continued)*

The Sharp Major Scales and Chords

Notice how the number of sharp symbols next to the bass clef in each of these examples increases as these scales go on. Again, the sharps near the clef indicate which notes will be played sharp (or one fret higher) throughout the piece of music.

D Major scale

D Major chord fingering

A Major scale

A Major chord fingering

E Major scale

E Major chord fingering

Notice in the C# Major scale that ALL of the notes are sharp, or played one fret up.

B Major scale

B Major chord fingering

F# Major scale

F# Major chord fingering

C# Major scale

C# Major chord fingering

CONTINUED ON NEXT PAGE

Major Chords and Scales *(continued)*

The Flat Major Scales and Chords

Like the sharp scales, notice how the number of flats goes up as these scales go on. These flats in the key signature again indicate which notes will be played one fret down for the duration of the piece.

B♭ Major scale

B♭ Major chord fingering

E♭ Major scale

E♭ Major chord fingering

A♭ Major scale

A♭ Major chord fingering

Practice these scales and fingerings and keep saying the notes to yourself as you play them. Pretty soon, you'll have all of these scales and chords memorized.

Note: *All of the notes in the C Flat Major scale are flat.*

D♭ Major scale

D♭ Major chord fingering

G♭ Major scale

G♭ Major chord fingering

C♭ Major scale

C♭ Major chord fingering

Minor Scales and Chords

Natural minor scales differ from major scales by only three notes. These notes give the minor scale a quality often described as sadder or darker than the major scales. It's easy to express these differences using the Roman numeral shorthand. Notice how the third, sixth, and seventh notes in the scale are shown as flat. This defines the minor scale.

Construct a Minor Chord

To make a minor chord, you still use the root note, the third, and the fifth of a scale. The difference between a minor chord and a major chord is that the third note is flat.

C	D	E♭	F	G	A♭	B♭	C
i	ii	III	iv	v	VI	VII	viii

Take a look at the A minor scale. Notice how the key signature for A minor is the same as C Major. This means that there are no sharps or flats in the A minor scale, just like the C Major scale. A minor is the *relative minor* scale to the C Major. Every major scale has a relative minor scale that begins three frets down from the root note.

A	B	C	D	E	F	G	A
i	ii	III	iv	v	VI	VII	viii

Here are the notes for the A minor scale, along with a recommended fingering.

A minor scale—index finger on lower A: E string

To make an A minor chord, play the root, the third, and the fifth notes of the minor scale (a). You could also use the sample fingering shown in b for A minor chord tones.

 a

A minor chord—index finger on lower A: E string

b

A minor chord—pinky finger on lower A: E string

Now take a look at some other minor scales and chords with sample fingerings. Remember that each minor scale is the relative minor of the major scale with the same key signature.

The Sharp Minor Scales and Chords

E minor scale

E minor chord fingering

B minor scale

B minor chord fingering

F# minor scale

F# minor chord fingering

C# minor scale

C# minor chord fingering

CONTINUED ON NEXT PAGE

G# minor scale

G# minor chord fingering

D# minor scale

D# minor chord fingering

Just like the C# Major scale, the A# minor scale contains all sharp notes.

A# minor scale

A# minor chord fingering

TIP

Chords are grouped into *chord progressions,* or a series of chords played over time. These chord progressions are the basis of the vast majority of songs you listen to today.

The Flat Minor Scales and Chords

D minor scale

D minor chord fingering

G minor scale

G minor chord fingering

C minor scale

C minor chord fingering

F minor scale

F minor chord fingering

CONTINUED ON NEXT PAGE

B♭ minor scale

B♭ minor chord fingering

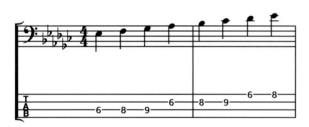

E♭ minor scale

E♭ minor chord fingering

As with the C♭ Major scale, the A♭ minor scale contains all flat notes.

A♭ minor scale

A♭ minor chord fingering

 TIP

Memorize, then forget

You'll want to be able to play these scales
without having to think too much about
what notes you're playing. Commit these
notes to memory, and then try to make
your playing as natural as possible.

Seventh Chords

The most common addition to major and minor chords is the seventh note, or the VII note, from each scale. The chords are the same, but each chord has four notes instead of three.

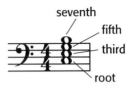

seventh
fifth
third
root

Major Seventh Chords

Start with the C Major seventh chord tones, along with a sample fingering.

The fingering is just the same as the C Major chord; however, you use your ring finger to play the seventh of the scale as well. Take a look at the rest of the major seventh chords now.

C Major seventh chord

G Major seventh chord

D Major seventh chord

A Major seventh chord

E Major seventh chord

B Major seventh chord

CONTINUED ON NEXT PAGE

F# Major seventh chord

C# Major seventh chord

F Major seventh chord

Bb Major seventh chord

Eb Major seventh chord

Ab Major seventh chord

Db Major seventh chord

Gb Major seventh chord

Cb Major seventh chord

Minor Seventh Chords

In addition to the notes in the typical minor chord, the minor seventh chord includes the flat seventh found in the minor scale.

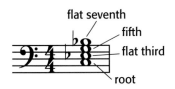

Create the A minor chord from the A minor scale. Look at this sample fingering above (right). Again, it's just an additional note to the familiar minor chord. Here are the additional minor seventh chords and fingerings.

E minor seventh chord

B minor seventh chord

F# minor seventh chord

C# minor seventh chord

G# minor seventh chord

D# minor seventh chord

CONTINUED ON NEXT PAGE

A♯ minor seventh chord

D minor seventh chord

G minor seventh chord

C minor seventh chord

F minor seventh chord

B♭ minor seventh chord

E♭ minor seventh chord

A♭ minor seventh chord

Seventh Chords

The last of the more common variety of seventh chords features the same notes as the major chords; however, the seventh note is flat. The chord is referred to as a seventh chord only. No major or minor terminology is used. The Roman numeral shorthand looks like this.

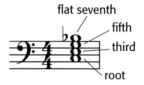

Take a look at the seventh chords. Notice how the seventh note is played one fret down from the C Major seventh chord.

C seventh chord

G seventh chord

D seventh chord

A seventh chord

E seventh chord

B seventh chord

CONTINUED ON NEXT PAGE

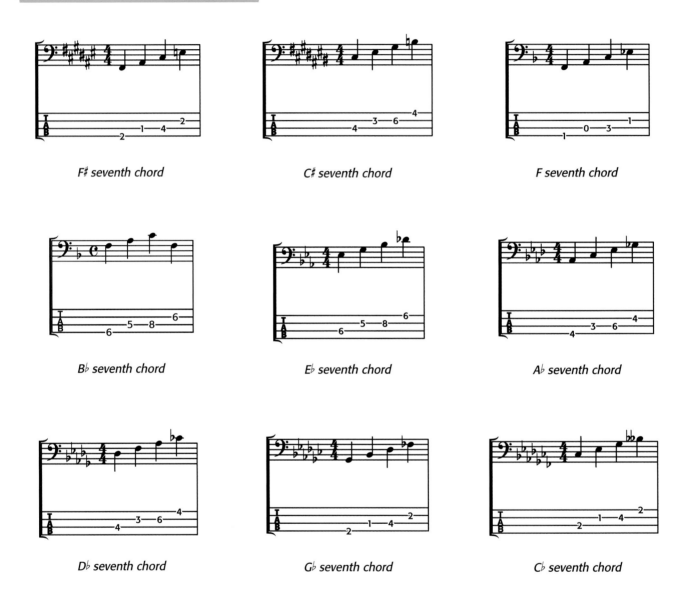

F# seventh chord

C# seventh chord

F seventh chord

B♭ seventh chord

E♭ seventh chord

A♭ seventh chord

D♭ seventh chord

G♭ seventh chord

C♭ seventh chord

You'll notice in the last example that there are some notes with two flat notes next to it. This *double flat* means that you'll lower the note a whole step from the natural note, instead of a half-step. This sums up a great deal of the chords you'll see while playing popular music. There are many different scales and chord types used in modern music—this book deals with the more commonly used ones. Other chord types add notes such as the sixth or the ninth (the second note played an octave higher). This book explains those types as it goes along.

Arpeggios

The proper word for playing the notes of the chord one at a time is *arpeggio* (*ar-pedge-ee-oh*), but you've already done this by playing the exercises in this chapter. Take these arpeggio exercises you've been playing and put them into actual song form.

Some Simple Songs

SIMPLE SONG IN C MAJOR

This song's bass line is built entirely on the arpeggios for the chords. The bass guitar's common role in music is to establish the root note and outline the chord, and this bass line takes care of that in a simple but effective way.

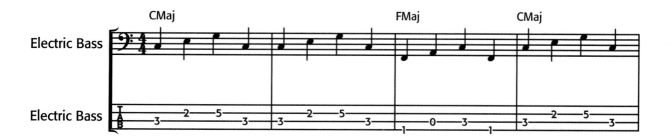

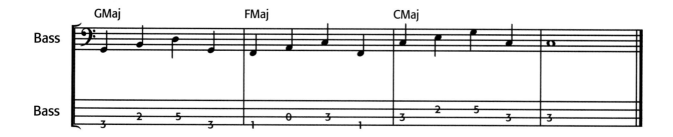

CONTINUED ON NEXT PAGE

Arpeggios
(continued)

SIMPLE SONG IN A MINOR

Now, take a look at a minor chord example.

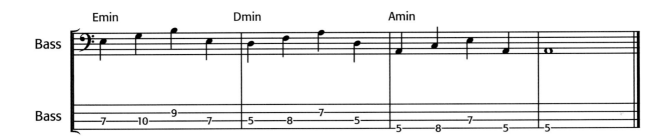

SIMPLE SONG IN G MAJOR

Finally, take a look at this simple song with a mixture of chords and arpeggio-based lines.

There are a few things to take note of in this bass line. First, although the song is in G Major, there are C seventh and D seventh chords in the song. There's also a note that falls outside the normal scale associated with G Major. In this case, the *B* has a flat symbol next to it to indicate that you play it one fret lower than normal. Again, this is known as an accidental (see Chapter 7), and it means that all *B* notes in that specific measure only are played flat. The *B* notes in any of the upcoming measures will be played as normal '*B*'s, unless they have the 'flat' accidental in front of them. Despite the different chords, these arpeggios outline the song and give it character and definition. At its heart, this outlining is the role of the bass guitar.

9

Common Chord Progressions

Although each song has its own character and personality, many tunes share a common backbone. By learning several common chord progressions, you can give yourself a head start in playing with other musicians. Although you'll encounter many different keys and chords, you'll still be ready to go.

Chord Symbols

You looked at Roman numerals in preceding chapters as a way of describing the individual notes in several different types of chords. Those numerals indicated the place in the scale where specific notes fell, depending on the key of the song. These same Roman numerals can also be used to describe the chords that occur in a song.

Expand Your Chord Knowledge

SAME STRUCTURE, DIFFERENT NOTES

By learning the overall structure of a song and understanding how to plug in different chords, you can easily recognize these chord progressions and learn new songs quickly. You can also transpose a song into a new key with a minimum of effort. This skill is especially valuable if you're dealing with a singer who might need to sing in a specific key. Just a quick adjustment, and you'll be able to play a wide variety of music with a wide variety of players. Note how the Roman numerals in the following example outline the chord progression of the music.

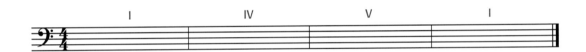

You're already familiar with the Roman numerals, so you can match up the chords in the key of C Major with the Roman numerals and see which chords are common.

C Major	D minor	E minor	F Major	G Major	A minor	B minor♭5
I	ii	iii	IV	V	vi	vii

These basic chords commonly show up in the key of C Major. If you expand on these chords using notes common to the C Major scale, you could expand the basics to the following extended chords.

C Major 7	D minor 7	E minor 7	F Major 7	G Major 7	A minor 7	B minor 7♭5
I	ii	iii	IV	V	vi	vii

There are a couple of things to notice in this last chart. First, chords with additional seventh notes in them are often abbreviated with a 7, as in C Major 7 or G7 (see Chapter 8 for more about seventh chords). Second, you'll also notice that there is a chord in that list with a ♭5 following it. In that case, the chord would have the fifth note in the scale played flat. For example, the notes in an E minor 7♭5 would be *E, G, B flat,* and *D*.

Let's take a look at the common chords found in the key of G Major.

G Major 7	A minor 7	B minor 7	C Major 7	D7	E minor 7	F minor 7♭5
I	ii	iii	IV	V	vi	vii

And now look at the common chords in F Major.

F Major 7	G minor 7	A minor 7	B♭ Major 7	C7	D minor 7	E minor 7♭5
I	ii	iii	IV	V	vi	vii

Notice in this last list of chords that there are flats in two different places, meaning two different things. The flat in the B♭ Major 7 chord refers to the naturally occurring fourth degree of the F Major scale: *B♭*, and the seventh chord that is built off of it. The flat in the E minor 7♭5 appears before the note in that chord that it modifies and refers only to that fifth note of the chord (in this case, again a *B♭*, the flattened fifth degree of a triad that is built off *E*, the seventh degree of the F Major scale).

BREAK IT DOWN

Musicians often abbreviate these chord names even further to save time writing and to pack as much information as possible into a small amount of space. For example, a major chord is often abbreviated as "Maj," and a minor chord is shortened to "min." So if you saw D♭min, you'd know that was a D minor chord. Add the number "7" to the end, and you'd get a D minor seventh chord. Notes in extended chords would come after these symbols, as in "Dmin7♭5." Refer to the following chart for reference.

CONTINUED ON NEXT PAGE

Abbreviation/Symbol	Meaning	Reference to Following Chord Examples
Maj	Major	a
min	minor	b
dim	diminished (chord with a flat third and a flat fifth)	c
sus	chord includes the fourth note of the scale, but not the third, giving the chord a 'suspended' feeling	d
aug	augmented (chord includes the root, a major third, and a sharp fifth)	e
♭5	flatted fifth	f
6	sixth	g
7	seventh	h
9	ninth (the second note of the chord's scale played an octave up). Tip: A major ninth can be added to all possible seventh chords for an interesting variation.	i
♯5	sharp fifth	This is another name for an augmented chord, so see e
♭9	flatted ninth	j
♯9	sharp ninth	k
11	The chord includes an eleventh (the fourth note of the scale played an octave up; i.e. root, minor third, fifth, flat seventh, ninth, eleventh)	l
♯11	The chord includes a sharp eleventh (root, major third, fifth, major seventh, ninth, sharp eleventh) Tip: Add a sharp 11th to major or dominant ninth chords (these include a flat seventh) for an interesting variation.	m
13	The chord includes a thirteenth (the sixth note of the chord's scale played an octave up; i.e. root, major third, fifth, flat seventh, major ninth, sharp eleventh, major thirteenth)	n

FAQ

There are a great many variations on harmony once you start using notes from the seventh and above. This book cannot discuss all of these possibilities, as many works have been dedicated to that subject alone. Look for more advanced books on music theory and harmony to study this subject further.

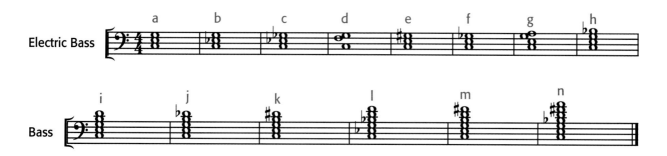

These abbreviations can be added to the Roman numerals to give more information to the basic structure. For example, a IImin7 chord just requires you to play the second note of the key's scale to get the chord you should be playing along to. If the key changes, the basic chord structure stays the same. Only the names of the notes have changed. The abbreviation gives you all the additional information to build from there.

These abbreviations are used in this and later chapters to show you common chord progressions. The job of the bassist is to keep the rhythm of these songs while playing the notes that outline the chords of the songs. By reading these chords, you'll know which notes belong in that chord and what you should be playing.

You usually find these chords named just above the staff as a reference point for the musicians. The next section shows you how to read these collections of symbols, commonly known as a *chart*.

Charts

This common shorthand for written music can include many elements; however, the most common feature of charts is the chord progressions of the song. Right now, the chords are shown centered above the measures. Later, you will see these chords the way they are usually listed—at the top-left of a measure.

What the Symbols Mean

There might not be any written notes on the staff, but the chord symbols above the staff let you know what notes are likely to be played in each measure (also known as a *bar*). In the example below, notice how there's no chord symbol above the second measure. That means that the chord symbol from the preceding measure applies to that one as well. In other words, this section of the song is made up of two bars of CMaj, one bar of FMaj, and one bar of G7.

This type of chart locks the chord progression into the key of C Major. However, you might also see a chord chart that looks like this example:

By looking at this chord progression, you know the basic information of the song you're playing. The only information you need at this point is the key of the song, which can change depending on the needs of the song or the performers. If you're given the key of B Major, the chords become BMaj7, F♯7, G♯min7, and EMaj. Change the key to D, and you get DMaj7, A7, Bmin7, and GMaj. This chord progression can be changed to whatever you need.

You can also take a series of specific chords and create a generic chart from there with a little work. Take a look at the C Major example used earlier and figure out the Roman numerals from there. From the key signature, you know that the CMaj chord is based on the root note, so you can give that chord the first Roman numeral. In the C Major scale, F is the fourth note, so that chord becomes IVMaj. G is the fifth note in that scale, so that chord becomes a V7. From there, you could write the example this way:

IMaj   IVMaj   V7

Electric Bass

You might also see some charts with multiple chord symbols over one bar. That means that there are two or more chords played during that measure. If you see something like this example, the first two beats of the measure use the first chord, whereas the second two beats use the second chord.

IImin   V7

Electric Bass

If there are slashes underneath the chords (as in the example above), the slashes indicate each beat in that measure. In the following example, the first chord is played over the first three beats, whereas the second chord is played over the fourth.

IImin   V7

Electric Bass

CONTINUED ON NEXT PAGE

So What Do I Play?

As mentioned before, these charts might or might not include actual written notes. If the notes are written, you know exactly what you're supposed to play at any point in time in the music, because the writer has a specific bass line in mind. If you don't have any written notes, or if you just have somebody telling you what chords to play, you have to make it up as you go along.

First, remember that the bassist's job is to define the basic harmony of the song. You can never go wrong playing the root of the chord, so always keep that note in mind as the first option. Whether it's GMaj or a Gmin7♭5, the root of the chord works.

From there, you can add chord tones or other notes to round out the bass part. There should always be some melodic content to the bass-line, even if it's just one well chosen note that leads melodically from one chord to the next. When adding these notes, keep in mind the rhythm of the song as well. Chapter 10 addresses common rhythms.

Honor these two commitments, and you'll put together a bass line that keeps the song interesting and holds down the rhythm and beat of the music for the other instruments.

With these two principles in mind, take a look at some common chord structures you're likely to run into as you play. With each example, try to look for the ways you could move, or *transpose,* these progressions to different keys. The notes might change, but the skeleton of the song remains the same.

The I-IV-V combination is one of the most common chord progressions in popular music today. From a basic blues song through early rock to today's pop music, you're likely to run into some variation of these chords.

The 12-Bar Blues

The name doesn't refer to the number of drinking establishments a musician is likely to visit in a weekend. The "bar" refers to the measures of the song, and the number "12" tells you how many bars are in the song. Those 12 bars are repeated over and over again until the song ends. At the end of the 12th bar, just go back to the beginning and play through it one more time.

Take a look at the Roman numeral layout for a common blues progression:

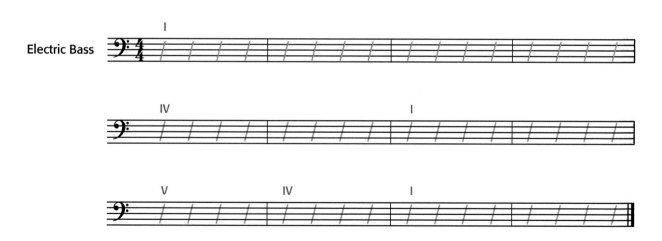

CONTINUED ON NEXT PAGE

This is the basic layout for a blues song. In the absence of any specifics to the chord, assume it's a major chord. Plug in a common key signature and see what those chords become.

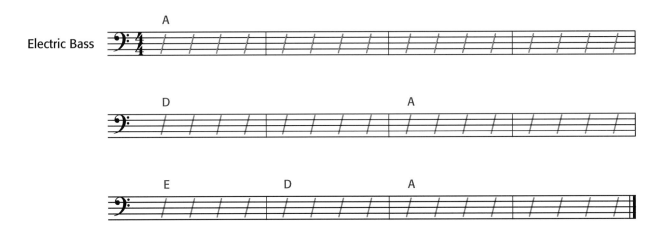

You're likely to see this key in the blues, because it's an easy one for guitars and basses to play in.

FACT

If you're looking for the history of the bass in blues music, there's really only one name to start with. Not only is Willie Dixon well respected as a bassist for artists like Muddy Waters, Howlin' Wolf, and Chuck Berry, but he also left a legacy as a songwriter and producer for Chess Records. He played the upright bass, but his songs and lines apply just as well to the bass guitar. Seek out one of the many versions of his songs (like "Spoonful") and be amazed at the legacy he's left to bassists and the blues in general.

Now, I'll go ahead and put in some notes to show you a common way to play a 12-bar blues progression. Notice how these notes both outline the chords in the progression and keep the rhythm of the song at the same time.

CONTINUED ON NEXT PAGE

Now take a look at the same progression in the key of D, with some additional chord information. The chords are a little different now, and there's a return to the V chord at the end of the song. This is a fairly common occurrence because it adds some more movement to the song and it indicates to both the listeners and the players that the progression is returning back to the beginning, or the *top,* of the song.

Take a look at a minor blues progression with a little more variation. Beyond the minor tonality of the song, there are more changes in the chords and more variety in the last bar of the song.

There are as many variations on blues progressions as there are people who play the blues, but this gives you a good idea of what to look for in a basic blues progression. Memorize these basic forms, and when somebody calls out a key, you'll be ready to go.

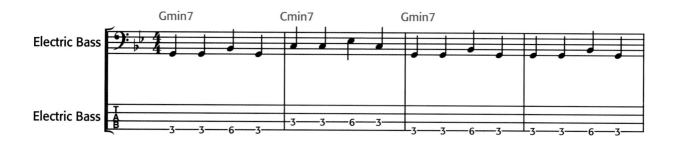

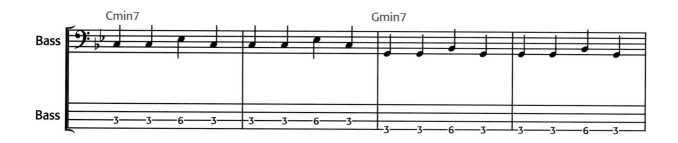

CONTINUED ON NEXT PAGE

Other I-IV-V Progressions

Blues songs aren't the only place you're likely to see these chords. For example, look at this progression with a 1960s British pop influence.

Play these notes with a quick, choppy style to emphasize that feel. In musical terminology, this is called a *staccato* feel (the dots under the notes indicate staccato). There is a precise beginning and end to each note. Notice how the chords are the same, but the structure and the notes change the feel of the song greatly.

You might also see this progression in different time signatures. The longer notes seem to make the progression glide along, and the time signature gives it a folksy feel, similar to a waltz.

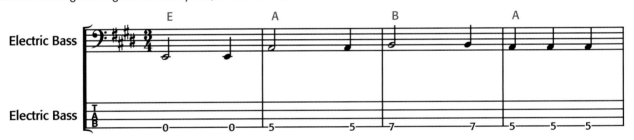

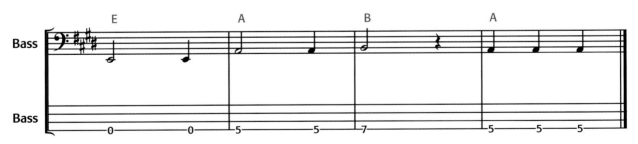

Play these notes with a longer, lingering style; in other words, hold them for their full count before releasing them to play the next note. Try to leave no gaps at all between notes. This is known as a *legato* feel. The notes almost seem to blend into each other.

No matter what styles or rhythms are applied to this progression, you'll find that this common progression shows up in many of your favorite songs. Once you make playing this structure familiar to your ears and your hands, you'll be ready to play a great deal of material.

Another common chord progression adds a minor chord to the familiar I-IV-V chords. It's a very natural progression, used extensively in rock and pop music from the '50s to today.

Adding a Minor Chord

The I-IV-V progression contains mainly major or seventh chords, at least in the major keys. In this progression, the vi chord naturally implies a minor tonality and often will be denoted by a minus sign next to it, i.e. VI–. For example, in the C Major scale, the vi chord would be A minor (the relative minor of the C Major scale). A sample I-vi-IV-V progression in C Major looks like this.

In the G Major scale, the progression looks like this.

In F Major, the I-vi-IV-V looks like this.

You can take these generic chords and apply them to every other major key and expand the chords from there. Again, the V naturally lends itself to a seventh chord (and is the naturally occurring seventh chord built off the fifth degree of every major scale), and the vi chord lends itself to a minor tonality (as a minor seventh chord is the naturally occurring seventh chord built off the sixth degree of every major scale).

CONTINUED ON NEXT PAGE

Following the Movement

This progression is a good time to look at using notes that lead from chord to chord in a song. A bassist uses these tones to indicate that a chord change is coming and to add interest to the song. Take a look at a sample of this chord progression with just the root notes written.

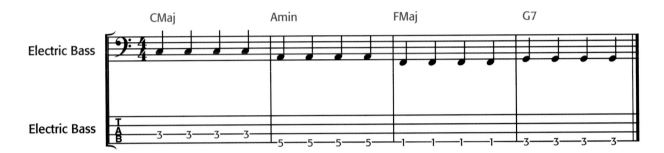

Now, take a look at this same example with the last notes changed to lead toward the next chord.

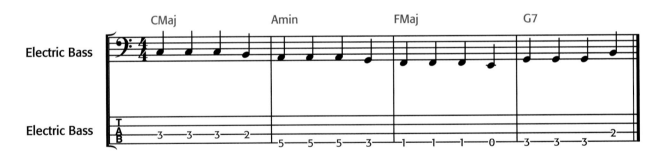

These leading tones indicate what the next chord will be. They come between the chord tones on the key's scale, so it sounds natural as you play these notes to get from chord to chord. It gives the bass line a sense of motion and interest, but it also maintains its responsibility to hold down the rhythm and tonality of the chord progression.

Take a look at this progression with some chord tones in addition to the leading tones.

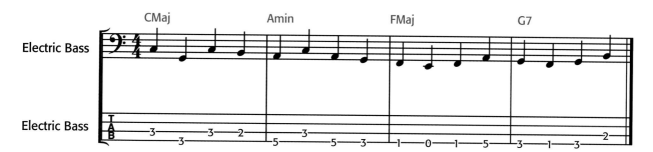

Notice in this case how the notes move in the opposite direction of the previous examples, but they still contain the same scale notes as the other examples. The notes are basically the same, but the direction makes it a different song.

Also look in this case at *passing tones,* or notes that don't necessarily appear in the scale but still add some interest and motion to the bass line.

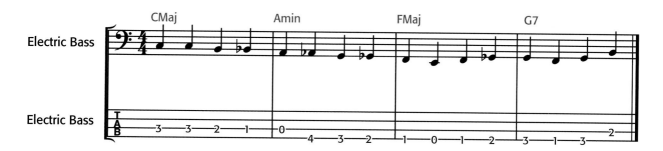

Even when the notes don't appear in the scale, they give the bass line some movement and make the music sound interesting. When a note falls outside the scale, it gives the song a little character and keeps it from sounding too structured or formal. Again, making sure that these notes are melodic and support the rest of the song are the things to keep in mind when choosing to use chromatic passing tones. Be judicious! Sometimes it's okay to break the rules.

More Chord Progressions

There are many ways to organize and present the chords in any given scale. Songwriters have had a lot of time to experiment with combinations of these chords to make new and different songs. Besides the progressions you've looked at up to this point (I-IV-V and I-vi-IV-V), there are some other common progressions that show up from time to time in songs.

Other Chord Progressions

II-V-I PROGRESSION

The ii-V-I progression doesn't often turn up as the main structure of a song. More often, it shows up in traditional jazz songs as what's called a *turnaround*, or a set of chord changes that indicates that the chord progression is returning to the beginning of the musical phrase that it's a part of.

Take a look at that progression in C Major.

Most often, the ii chord implies a minor chord, whereas the V implies a seventh chord. This progression could also be played this way.

In a minor key, the ii-V-I could be played this way.

The ii chord is still minor, although the fifth note in that chord is played flat. The V chord remains a seventh chord and the I chord remains minor. Getting the sound of this turnaround in your head helps you play a great many songs.

I-VI-II-V PROGRESSION

This progression (I-vi-ii-V) adds another minor chord to the ii-V-I progression and gives it a little more movement. This progression might also sound familiar, although a little "old-timey."

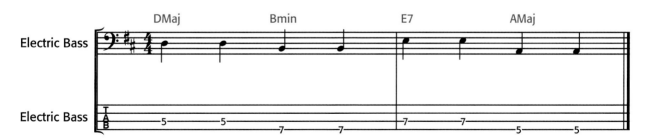

Don't always look for those patterns. Songs can have chord progressions that move up in half- or whole-steps, and some chords might not even have notes beyond the root and fifth notes (this is often referred to as a *power chord*, and it's especially popular with rock and metal guitarists). So although not all songs follow these simple patterns mentioned above, these patterns are really important and common building blocks in many, many songs. Looking for these patterns will help you see when they occur and help you develop your ear to hear not only them, but other chords besides.

chapter **10**

Basic Rhythms

A pop song, a reggae song, and a jazz song can have the same chord progressions and notes. It's the rhythm of each song that gives it character and personality. Part of the bass guitar's responsibility is defining that rhythm, and this chapter breaks down the basic concepts of rhythm and how to improve your natural sense of time: musician-speak for *sense of timing and rhythm*. It also gives you several different examples of the rhythms unique to many genres of music, so you'll be better prepared to play whatever type of music you love.

The Metronome

Throughout all of the exercises in this book, the metronome is both your guide and your traffic cop. This device provides a clear, steady, and uncluttered beat for you to play along with. By practicing with the metronome, you get a good sense of the beat's exact location and what you need to work on.

How to Use the Metronome

The metronome produces a click on every beat at the speed you set. Usually, this ranges from somewhere around 70 to 220 *bpm,* or *beats per minute.* For reference, you'll find that most dance music falls around 120 bpm, whereas most ballads and slow music range from 85 to 95 bpm. Fast rock comes in around 145 bpm and up, and you'll find speeds upward of 180 bpm in genres such as speed metal and punk.

The most common way to use the metronome is to play on every beat the metronome plays. Try this exercise to get comfortable with playing on the beat.

1 Set the metronome speed to 90 bpm.

2 Fret the *C* note on the *A* string.

③ Play a *C* on each click of the metronome.

④ When you feel comfortable at that tempo, move up the tempo in 5 bpm increments.

The metronome beat seems to disappear when you're playing directly on the beat. If you hear the click happening before or after you play the note, you need to bring your playing back in line with the tempo. If you're playing before the click, you're playing too quickly. If you're playing after the click, you're playing too slowly. Adjust your speed accordingly.

For all of the exercises in this book, play along with the metronome and concentrate on maintaining the correct tempo as you play. You'll develop a better sense of rhythm and time as you go.

TIP

Before you start to play, try listening to the metronome and count the tempo along with the click. This helps you internalize the rhythm and better understand the beat.

Quarter Notes

Now that you're familiar with the workings of the metronome and how to play along with it, start out with some basic quarter-note rhythms. You should already be familiar with these because these steady notes are what you practiced with the scales and chords earlier in this book.

Quarter-Note Rhythms

Play the following example to get used to playing with a chord change and the metronome at the same time. Remember, start slow (at around 95 bpm) and go up from there only after you're able to play all of the notes clearly and consistently.

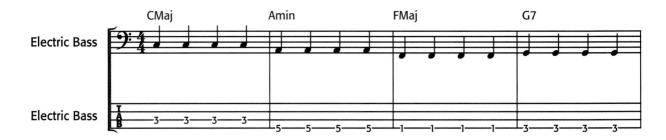

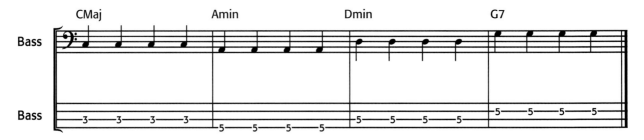

In the example at the top of the next page, there's a rest on the second beat of each measure. That means that you don't play a note on the second beat of each bar; however, the tempo of the other notes must remain the same. Get used to leaving some space while playing, and don't anticipate playing the third beat in the measure. The chord change is also a little different.

TIP

Rhythm is as much a function of what you don't play and where as what notes you choose to play. Remember that a little extra space in the right place makes the song move along and gives it character.

Electric Bass

Electric Bass

Bass

Bass

If you play on the first and third beats, as in the exercise that follows, you'll get a familiar sound. This type of rhythm is used in different genres of music the world over, from country to polka. It's a good idea to get used to playing this one because you're liable to use it a great deal in whatever type of music you choose to play.

Electric Bass

Electric Bass

Bass

Bass

CONTINUED ON NEXT PAGE

Now take out the notes on beats two and three. There's a lot more space in the music; the note on the fourth beat serves almost to announce the next measure.

Finally, try the following example in 3/4 time. There are three quarter notes per measure here. You'll likely find this feel in waltzes or folk music, along with some jazz songs.

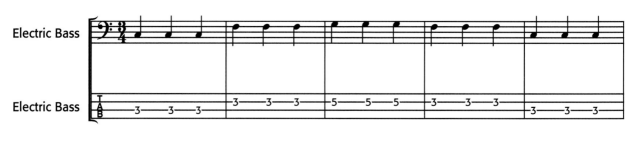

Each of these examples gets you used to playing along with the metronome and feeling a rhythm beyond what the clicks are playing. Practice these in several different tempos to get used to them and feel how they change at different speeds.

As the name implies, there are eight of this type of note in a 4/4 measure of music. In odd-meter tempos, such as 3/4 or 5/4, there are double the top number of these notes per measure. If the emphasis of the time signature is on eighth notes, such as 6/8 or 12/8, there are as many eighth notes as the top number in the time signature. Remember overall that the upper number represents the number of beats in a measure, and the lower number represents the note value that receives one beat.

Straight Eighth-Note Rhythms

In this example, you play two notes per beat, as shown by the count underneath the notes. Make sure each note gets an equal amount of time when you play.

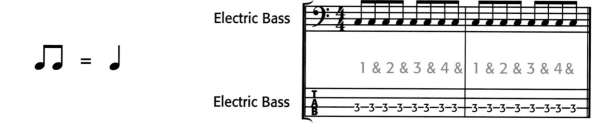

Start with the bpm setting on the metronome at around 85 and work your way up from there. Straight eighth notes are a common feature of rock music, where the rhythm gives the song a driving force. Try it with a C Major scale, using two eighth notes for each note of the scale.

1️⃣ Start at around 85 bpm and go faster from there.

2️⃣ Try moving other scales into similar eighth-note patterns.

3️⃣ Count the beats out loud to help you keep track of where you are. Say "one-and-two-and-three-and-four" where the numbers fall on the beat of the metronome.

4️⃣ Move on only when each note is clear and distinct.

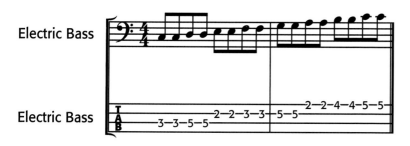

CONTINUED ON NEXT PAGE

Eighth Notes
(continued)

Follow the same directions in playing the scale with just one eighth note per note of the scale.

Electric Bass

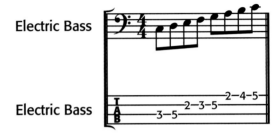

Electric Bass

Also play the arpeggios from previous examples in eighth-note patterns, as shown in this example.

Electric Bass

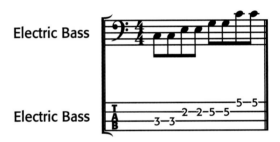

Electric Bass

Now put some rests in the exercises. In this example, play two eighth notes on the first and third beats. Keep counting the beats out loud, but play notes only when you say "one-and" and "three-and."

Pay close attention to the beat count in this next example. Notice where the rests fall in each grouping of four eighth notes. Give each note and rest its full value, so that it seems that the fourth eighth note is anticipating the next note.

Give this example a little bit more space. Count out the beats and play only

① Beat 1

② The "and" of beat 2

③ Beat 3

④ The "and" of beat 4

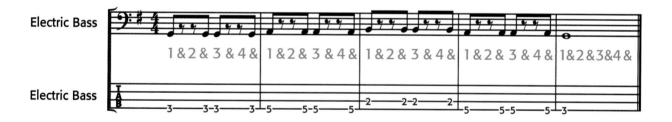

Again, the eighth notes on the "and" beats anticipate the main beats, a common occurrence in many popular styles of music. Remember to give each note and rest its proper value.

CONTINUED ON NEXT PAGE

Eighth Notes
(continued)

Dotted Eighth-Note Rhythms

If you were to hold the first eighth note until it was time to play the next eighth note, elongating the value, it would be written out like this:

Notice the dot following the quarter note. A *dotted* note means it gets an additional one-half-beat value. Therefore, a dotted quarter note receives the same value as three eighth notes.

You often see these kind of notes in pop or folk music, where the dotted quarter notes provide a solid foundation and the eighth notes often signal a change to a new chord. Look at this example in a familiar chord progression to get the feel. Again, count the beats out loud.

Try playing this example that includes dotted quarter notes and straight eighth-note sections as well.

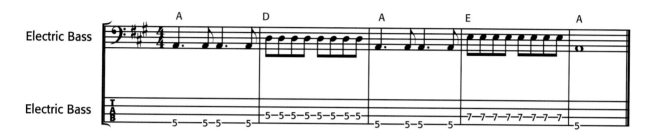

Eighth notes are also commonly found in three-note groups, or *triplets*. This means that although the beat count doesn't change—in this case a 4/4 time signature—the music gets almost a 3/4 feel over that beat count. You play three notes per metronome click in the following example. Take a look at this diagram to help get this triplet feel.

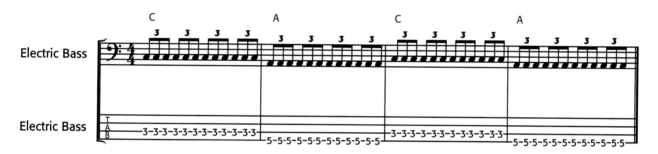

This might seem familiar to those who have heard Irish or Scottish folk music. It's similar to the feel of some blues songs, although that feel is more commonly not 12/8 time, where each eighth note gets its own beat.

You'll also run into cases where note values are combined to create some rhythmic interest; however, they'll be written with *ties.* Ties link two or more notes, putting all of their beat values together while keeping the notation in a familiar written form.

Try this exercise to get the feel of tied notes. Start slow and count out each note until you get the feel of the passage down.

CONTINUED ON NEXT PAGE

You'll also see instances where notes are tied across measure lines, so that the note carries across the first beat of the next bar. Look at this example, again starting slow and counting out loud each eighth note.

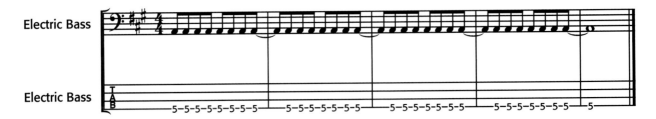

Combine the two examples, and you get something that feels like this:

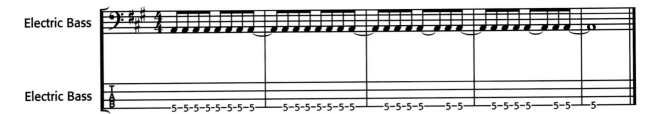

FACT

Practice this and count out the beats until this style of playing becomes natural to you. Eventually, you'll be able to stop counting the beats and just play this rhythm correctly.

This musical example has a *syncopated* feel to it, in that beats that don't normally receive emphasis are doing so now. Syncopation is a standard feature of modern popular music, so learning to shift the emphasis in rhythms to other beats is an important skill for a bassist.

An even smaller subdivision of rhythm is the sixteenth note. As you can probably tell by the name, 16 of these can be found per one 4/4 measure of music. If your music has an odd time signature, such as 3/4 or 7/4, multiply the top number by 4 to get the maximum number of sixteenth notes. If the time signature is based on eighth notes, as in 6/8, just multiply the top number by two. There are time signatures based on sixteenth notes, but they are rare.

Sixteenth-Note Rhythms

Four sixteenth notes equal two eighth notes, equal one quarter note.

It's important to start slow in this next example because you play four notes per beat in this example. It's essential that you start out playing this cleanly and evenly because it's easy to develop bad habits and then gloss over them by just speeding up the tempo. Keep this in mind as you play.

- Each note should be clear.
- Each note should get the same amount of time.
- Use precise fingering or picking while playing. Make sure that you strictly alternate your index and middle fingers or your up-and-down picking strokes with your plucking hand.
- Start at a bpm setting of around 75 on your metronome and work your way up from there.

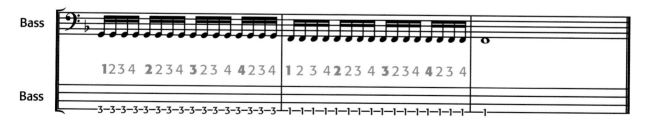

CONTINUED ON NEXT PAGE

Sixteenth Notes *(continued)*

It might help to count out the beats as you play. Try saying "One-e-and-a-Two-e-and-a" and so on as you go. Again, this helps you internalize the beat as you go, so that eventually you feel the beat without having to count it out.

Now apply these sixteenth-note rhythms to scales. In this case, start with the A minor scale. Play the ascending A minor scale with four sixteenth notes per scale note, as shown in this example.

1 Start with the metronome set at around 75 bpm.

2 Count out each beat while you play.

3 Make sure each note is clear and distinct.

4 Try the other scales as you progress through this exercise.

Try the arpeggios for each chord as well, following the same guidelines as in the preceding example. (See Chapter 8 for a refresher on arpeggios.) Start with the A minor arpeggio and go from there.

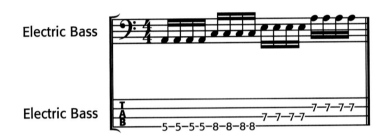

As you might imagine, sixteenth notes and their corresponding rests come and go pretty quickly. In this example, keep counting out the beats but don't play where the rests are indicated. This piece starts easily enough by just playing the first two sixteenth notes in each four-note group.

This approach emphasizes the beginning of each beat, making the music passage seem very quick and intense. By adding in another sixteenth note, it eases the music along a little and makes it seem a little more flowing.

More Dotted Rhythms

You'll often see dotted eighth notes along with sixteenth notes, with each dotted eighth note taking the place of three sixteenth notes.

$$\eighthnote. = \eighthnote\eighthnote\eighthnote$$

From rock to pop to metal, you're likely to encounter passages that look something like this:

CONTINUED ON NEXT PAGE

You can also invert the note groupings to give the passage a feel like the one shown here:

Compare that feeling to straight sixteenth notes in this example:

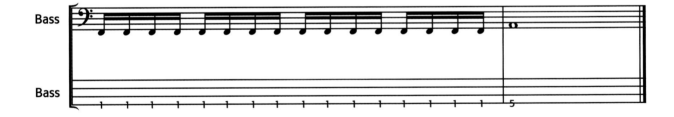

Count out each beat until you're familiar with how that rhythm feels. Now add in some straight eighth notes to compare those feels.

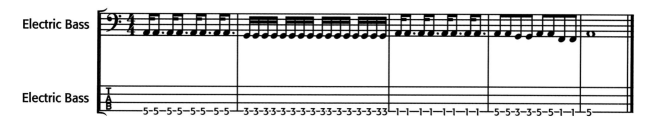

This grouping of eighth notes and sixteenth notes is also common. It alternates between sixteenth and eighth notes quickly, but it retains a straight beat count. Keep counting out loud and it should be easy to remember.

CONTINUED ON NEXT PAGE

That feel can also be reversed, as shown in this example:

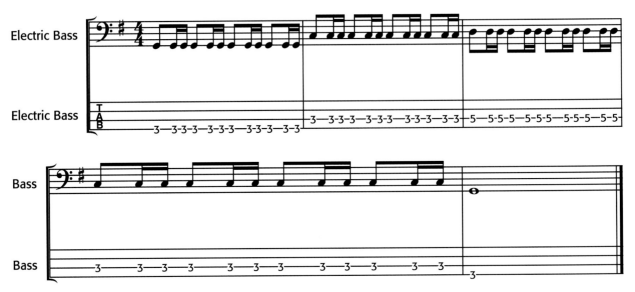

This example is a little tricky; however, keep counting the beats out loud and realize that the eighth note in the middle is just like combining two sixteenth notes.

Now try the sixteenth notes over a 3/4 time signature. Keep counting out the beats, but realize that there are only three groups of four sixteenth notes per measure.

Finally, try this sixteenth-note example using ties that cross the bar lines.

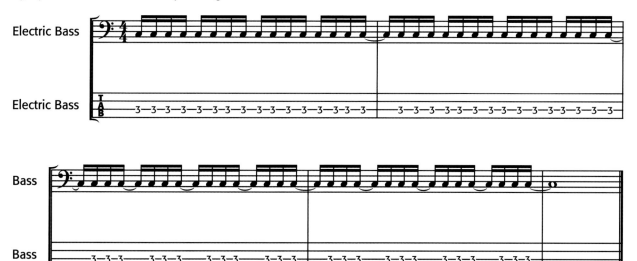

Sixteenth notes are usually the smallest subdivision of rhythm in most popular music. Remember that no matter what you run across, everything can be counted as a part of the overall rhythm, and that these rhythms feel more natural the more you practice them. Repeated practice helps you greatly here as the more you play these rhythms, the more you internalize them.

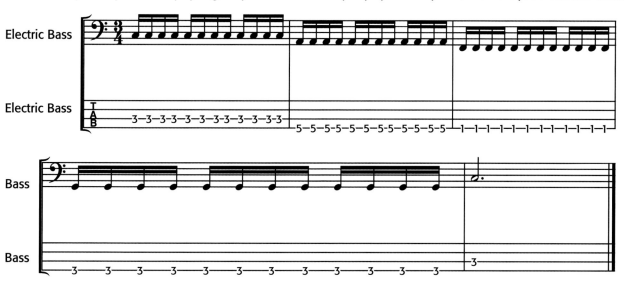

Applying Rhythms to Songs

Each genre of music has types of rhythms that are closely associated with its basic nature. When you hear these rhythms, it's easy to associate these songs with a certain kind of music. Changing a song's rhythm can quickly give it a new personality, even more so than changing the key of the song.

How to Distinguish Rhythms

Think of the difference when you give a heavy rock song a slower, reggae rhythm. The notes might not have changed, but it's certainly a different piece of music now. That's why learning several different rhythms makes you a more well-rounded player. You'll be ready for many different musical situations if you can convincingly play different rhythms. Following these steps helps you get a better idea of what's going on inside the song.

LISTEN

By exposing yourself to several different types and styles of music, you're hearing these rhythms in action. It's like a case study of what to play and what to avoid. Through careful listening, you get a sense of what tempos and rhythms work best in what styles of music. You also get a better sense of what separates certain genres of music, and what closely relates them.

Because jazz and blues share common roots, you might see some commonalities. Reggae rhythms have a fairly unique identity apart from country music, so you can learn something from that as well. Listen closely and learn the traits.

COUNT IT OUT

When it comes down to it, every rhythm can be broken down to a series of numbers. Whether it's easy to count out or it takes some time to dissect, you should be able to count out the number of beats per measure.

It might seem elementary, but clapping or counting out loud along with the song gives you a good indication of where the beats are and how many there are per measure. When you know where the major beats lie, you are better able to analyze the smaller rhythms inside the song.

FEEL IT

As you listen to each type of music, take note of how each rhythm feels and even makes you want to move. You'll know you're playing the rhythm right when you get that same feeling. Even with all the counting, it's really how the rhythm feels that you want to capture accurately.

Walking Bass

Walking bass is the slang term given to playing a steady quarter-note rhythm throughout the entire song. The term *walking* comes from the strong and purposeful notes played by the bass, like somebody walking steadily, through the entire song.

WHERE YOU WALK

Walking bass is most often found in jazz, where the steady rhythm and the ability to easily outline chords give songs a stable foundation for other musicians to improvise over. However, it's also useful in styles such as blues or rock where a solid base is helpful as well.

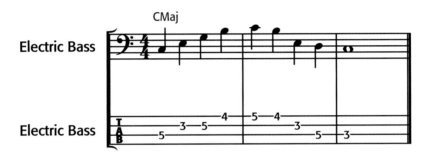

The example above shows two important functions of the walking bassline. It outlines the chord being played and it provides a steady rhythm to the music.

YOUR FIRST STEPS

When you first start learning to walk a bass line, it's a good idea to start with the root of the chord as your first note in any measure. This firmly establishes the chord being played. From there, it's usually a good idea to play a strong chord tone, like the third or fifth note of the arpeggio, on the third beat of the measure to further emphasize the chord. On beats two and four, you can either choose other chord tones, or choose notes called *passing tones* that aren't chord tones and don't necessarily even work with the chord but give the bass line direction (either up or down) and make it a little more interesting.

Look at this simple blues progression and follow this walking bass line to demonstrate these concepts.

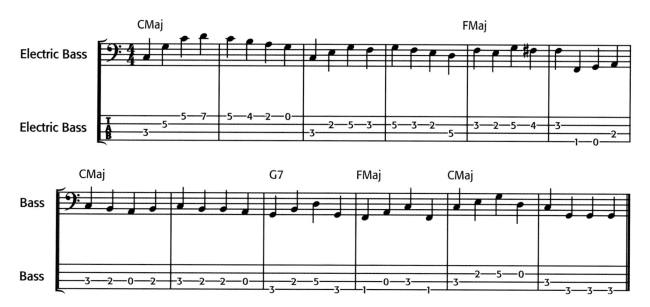

- Notice how the first note in the first measure is *C,* emphasizing the root of the chord.
- The chord tones lead toward the octave note of *C* at the beginning of the second measure.
- The notes are different in the third and fourth measure, but the general character of the line remains the same.
- Notice how the notes in the fourth measure lead up to the chord change in the fifth measure.
- After two measures of walking in *F,* the bass line leads back to *C.*
- The line walks through the rest of the song using the same principles, going through more bars of *C, G,* and *F.*
- Notice how the notes in the last measure don't resolve the chord, but instead indicate that the form is getting ready to repeat itself.

This simple line gives you a good example of how to walk a bass line through a simple chord progression. Remember that this isn't the only way to play a walking bass line, however. In fact, part of the appeal of a walking bass line is that it's usually never the same way twice. The bassist can change the direction of the bass line to fit the direction of a soloist, or he or she can make subtle changes to the chords to make things a little more interesting. There are no hard-and-fast rules to playing a walking bass line, so play around with it and see what sounds good and what you should avoid.

CONTINUED ON NEXT PAGE

The next example uses a different chord structure and adds some rhythmic variation to the line. Although the emphasis is still on the quarter-note pulse, there are small rests and sixteenth notes that propel the bass line. It gives the part a little spice without disrupting the overall groove.

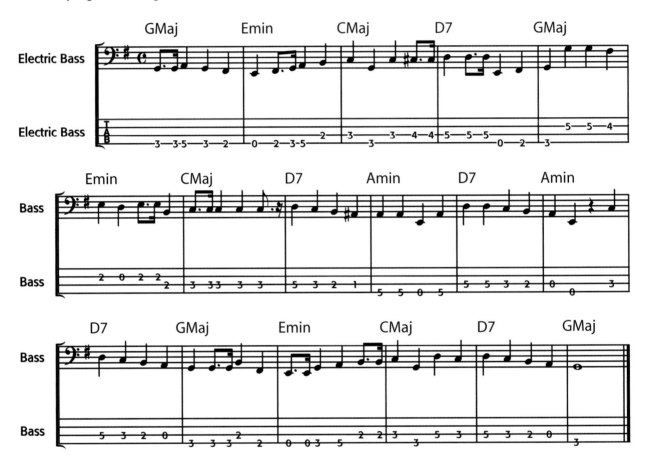

- Again, the *G* at the beginning of the song defines the chord, but the chord changes come a little bit more quickly in this song.
- Because the chords change more quickly, the line moves from one chord to the next and leads the other instruments more directly.
- The rhythmic variations tend to center around dotted eighth notes and sixteenth notes.
- This song has A and B sections. The A section follows a IMaj-VImin-IVMaj-V7 pattern, whereas the B section follows a IImin-V7 structure. The overall song follows an A-B-A pattern.
- Notice how the last measure of the song resolves to the root of the chord, helping to signal the end of the song.

Compared to the first example, this line has a little bit more *swing*. Swing is a term that's hard to define, but you'll know when you hear it. It's loosely based on a triplet feel; however, the notes aren't played exactly on that kind of count. The only way to accurately convey the feel of swing is to listen to classic examples of it. Find music by Count Basie, Duke Ellington, Dizzy Gillespie, Charlie Parker, and Miles Davis from the 1940s through the 1960s to start with, and you'll get a good idea of how swing should sound. Especially pay attention to recordings featuring bassists such as Paul Chambers, Ron Carter, and Ray Brown. They are masters of swing.

This last example follows two II-V-I patterns strung together, the first in A and the second in G. Notice that although the root doesn't change from one chord to the next, the notes surrounding those root tones do. Pay attention to how the chords shift and how the bass line handles it.

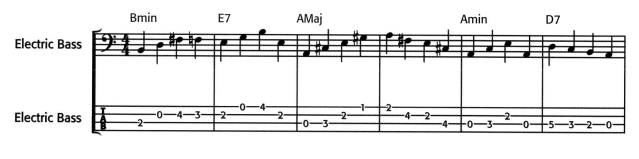

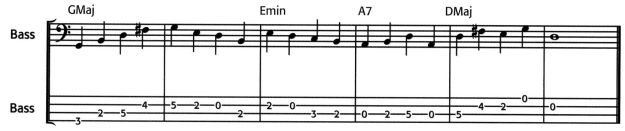

- This example is different because the chord doesn't start on the key of the song. Still, the first note identifies the chord. Songs don't always have to start on the key of the song.

- When the chord changes around the same root note, it's important to emphasize the notes that aren't shared by the chords. Play the third and seventh notes to outline the change.

The art of walking a bass line is a topic too vast to cover in one chapter, and many books and videos have been devoted to analyzing it. This gives you a good start in walking, however, and practicing these concepts will aid you greatly along the way.

Blues Shuffle

A style related to the swing feel, but with its own character, is the blues shuffle. Not all blues songs feel like this; however, it's a common rhythm, and one that you should get under your fingers in the beginning.

Get It Down

Although these kinds of lines are usually written in eighth notes for the sake of convenience, you should read the rhythm as groups of triplet eighth notes with the first two notes tied. Don't try to be extremely precise with the triplets; instead, give the first eighth note in each group a little more time than the second one. Practice this rhythm with the metronome beginning at around 90 bpm.

When you've got the shuffle feeling down, look at the following examples of full songs. These are typical patterns for the blues shuffle feel. They still outline the chords of the songs; however, the lines are more repetitious than those found in walking bass lines. When you've learned the pattern, you just have to move it from chord to chord to keep the song going. It's an easy concept, but it's essential that you have the feeling of the rhythm down to make the song sound right.

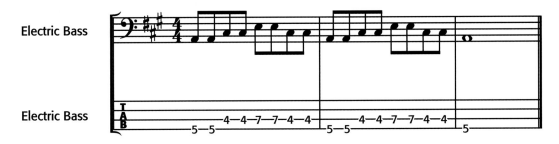

There's less variation in these kinds of bass lines than in walking bass lines; however, feel free to add some small rhythmic or harmonic variations as you go through. Although you have to keep the song's structure intact, there's room for *fills*, or small changes at the end of sections of the songs. They add a little variety to the bass line, and they can also serve to show when one part of the song is ending and another is beginning. In this way, they're almost a signal to the other musicians that something is going to change, so they should be ready for it.

Blues Shuffle Examples

The first example is pretty straightforward. Start out at a slower tempo and work your way up. This type of rhythm works at all tempos. When you play it quickly, it takes on an almost bouncing feel. When you play it slow, the rhythm takes on a dragging nature characteristic of the blues.

- Notice how the pattern repeats itself throughout the song.
- The pattern still outlines the chord notes, although it avoids notes such as the third and sixth in each scale. The seventh note is a common feature in blues patterns, although it's usually flat and not a major.
- Keep the shuffle feel going through the song. You and the drummer are responsible for making sure a smooth and steady shuffle is maintained.
- Notice how the last measure goes to the V7 chord again. This chord indicates a turnaround back to the beginning of the pattern.

Keeping this pattern consistent and even through the song is your goal.

CONTINUED ON NEXT PAGE

Blues Shuffle
(continued)

This next example highlights some small rhythmic variations and shows where fills can be used.

- The chords are now minor instead of seventh chords, and the darker nature of the pattern is emphasized by regularly using the flatted fifth note.
- By inserting more sixteenth notes into the pattern, the rhythms are a little more interesting.
- There are a couple of additional chord changes in this pattern. These substitutions are typical of blues songs, and you should get used to hearing these variations.
- Notice how there are more variations in the bass line at the ends of measures 4, 9, and 10. These fills help indicate changes coming on and add some interest to the song.

As you might have noticed in the last two examples, the major and minor thirds aren't stressed in the previous examples. Seventh chords are more common, where the major nature of the third note is tempered by the flat seventh in the chord. Minor chords also work especially well.

This last example demonstrates a compund time signature often found in the blues. Don't worry about the change too much, however. This 12/8 feel is a natural progression from the shuffle rhythms you've learned so far in this section. The triplet feel over a steady pulse even remains the same, although the emphasis is on eighth notes in groups of three now. Keep counting the rhythm in four beats, but give each beat three eighth notes.

- Notice how the dotted quarter notes each seem to occupy one beat. This sets the feel for the rest of the song.
- The note patterns change from dotted quarter notes to quarter and eighth notes in the second section of the song. Keep the shuffle feel here.
- The song moves away from 12 bars to 8 bars. This is another common variation on the blues form, so learn to play along with this at different tempos as well.

The blues has been around for quite awhile, so there are many more variations to learn. If you want to pick up more, listen to classic blues bassists such as Willie Dixon and newer masters such as Tommy Shannon to get an idea of what's possible.

Rock

The bass guitar usually plays two roles in rock music. As in other genres, it can play a supportive role through an individual bass part. Or it can play the same basic part as the guitar. That part is known as a *riff*, or a repetitive figure or part that makes up a section of the song.

What Distinguishes Rock Bass

STRAIGHT EIGHTH NOTES

The following example shows a simple but common type of bass line in rock music. As opposed to the shuffle feel of the blues, these eighth notes should be played exactly as written. Play this section repeatedly, increasing the tempo as you go.

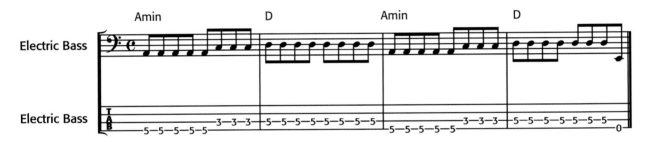

- At slower tempos, try practicing this section with a staccato feel and palm muting. This is a common usage in rock music.
- As you speed up, make sure to give each note equal value.
- The guitar could be doing several different parts over this kind of bass line. No matter what happens, it's important to maintain the consistent pulse and feel.
- The end of the bar of *D* in this bass line would be a good place to practice possible fills. Try playing additional notes, such as *A* or *G*, in this section to give it a little variety. Maintain the eighth-note pulse in any case, no matter what other notes you play.

At the top of the next page, you'll find a good example of a bass line that maintains its own pulse, independent of what the guitar is playing. View this next example as an independent bass line from the early days of rock and roll. This part would be at home in Fifties rock and roll or rockabilly styles.

- As with the preceding example, play these eighth notes straight, without a shuffle feel.
- This pattern outlines more of the chord than the preceding pattern, but it still allows the guitar to play a different part.
- This pattern doesn't allow for as many fills. It's important to keep this feel consistent.

These two examples give you a good idea of how to drive along a bass line in a rock song, be it a classic or a more modern tune. When building your own rock bass line, it's a good idea to stick to the root in the beginning; but you can expand from there to notes within the chord.

CONTINUED ON NEXT PAGE

RIFFS

The riff has been used from the classic rock of Led Zeppelin to the more modern rock and metal of Metallica and others. If you've heard songs like "Iron Man," "Sunshine of Your Love," and "Smoke on the Water," you've heard classic examples of the riff. The guitar and the bass guitar join together to play a single repetitive figure in a song, making the pattern seem that much bigger.

In most cases, the guitar plays a single note line or simple chords for this riff, and the bass guitar plays the root notes of that guitar line. If the guitarist starts a solo or another rhythm part, the bass guitar usually sticks with the riff, although it might add some more notes or slight rhythmic variations to fill out some of the space in the song.

Take a look at this riff and imagine a guitarist playing along with you.

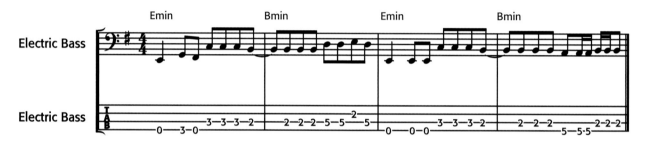

- Notice how the pattern extends beyond one measure.
- This pattern is in a minor key; however, you can see riffs that follow many different keys and chord structures.
- Concentrate on playing this example as precisely as possible. Remember, you're likely to play it with other musicians.
- Once you've got the basic riff down, you can experiment with fills and variations. This is useful if you're playing the riff by yourself, during a solo section for another instrument. Keep the basic structure of the riff down, however. You want to maintain the song, not fly off the handle.

This next example is a bit trickier. There are additional rests and quicker notes in this example. Again, make sure that you learn it exactly because you're going to be playing with other musicians and you want to sound as tight as possible.

- Count along with this beat as you play to keep your place. The placement of the rests can throw you off.
- Again, this example is in a minor key. Notice how the flat sixth notes in the riff give it a darker and edgier tone. This is a staple of hard rock and metal.

The riff's use of rests gives the rhythm *syncopation,* which means that the riff emphasizes beats other than the first and third beats in a measure. It's something you hear in the vast majority of rock music, as well as other genres such as R&B, blues, and jazz.

LISTEN UP

The term "rock music" includes everything from Elvis Presley to Nirvana. All of its various subgenres and divisions makes for a dizzying amount of music lumped under one name. These lines don't begin to explore the genius of bassists such as Paul McCartney, John Entwhistle, Geddy Lee, John Paul Jones, and many others, each with their own individual quirks and styles.

Although your goal should be eventually to sound like your own player instead of a clone of another famous musician, it's important to listen to your favorite music and try to understand what the bassist is doing in these songs. Whether they're playing their own line or riffing along with the guitarist, find out why and how they did it. It'll make you a better player.

R&B

Although the letters stand for "rhythm and blues," R&B has gone on to define much more than just a combination of bluesy sounds and steady rhythms. R&B includes classic soul, funk, and modern R&B songs under one large umbrella.

What Distinguishes R&B Bass

SOUL

The best in soul music stretches from the Motown sounds of Detroit through the famous Stax rhythm section in Memphis through Alabama's Muscle Shoals. Take a look at these examples to get a feel for what's going on in soul music.

- This bass line has a swing to it similar to jazz or blues. Remember that feel when you play the line.
- Soul music is based on syncopation, so remember to count out the beat to keep the time.
- This music is bouncy and happy (most of the time). Keep that emotion in mind as you play.

FACT

Some Famous R&B Bassists
- James Jamerson
- Donald "Duck" Dunn
- David Hood
- Chuck Rainey
- George Porter, Jr.
- Jerry Jemmot
- Bob Babbitt
- Tommy Cogbill

The preceding is an example of how a Motown bass line might sound. The next line an example of Memphis soul.

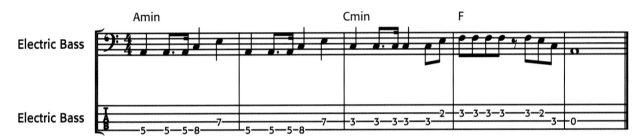

- This example also has a swing and bounce to it. Make sure it comes through in your playing.
- Soul music often relies on a deeper bass line with less high end. Try rolling off some of the tone on your bass guitar to see how that kind of music sounds.

The bass guitar is the heart of soul music. Play these lines smoothly to capture that feel.

FUNK

From James Brown and George Clinton through Prince and Rick James to its modern incarnation as part of hip-hop, funk relies more than any other genre on the bass guitar to propel it. Funk makes extensive use of rests and syncopation, and there's a constant emphasis on the "one," or the beginning of each measure.

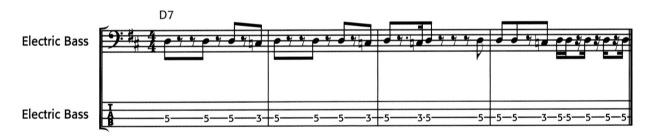

This bass line incorporates some of the attributes found in the music of James Brown.

- It looks simple, but the amount of space and the syncopation in the later parts of the measure make it tricky.
- The main action of the part takes place on the first beat of each measure. Make sure you hit those notes with conviction.
- The amount of space leaves room for sparing fills, but be careful not to overplay. You must maintain the groove.

CONTINUED ON NEXT PAGE

This line is a little busier and owes more to Eighties artists.

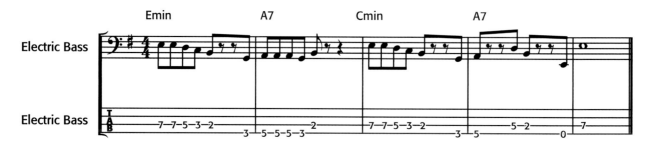

- This figure stretches across two measures, which adds to the syncopation of the part.
- Again, most of the emphasis lies on the first part of the music.
- This is a driving part, so don't be afraid to play it with a little attitude.
- Notice that this example is driven by eighth notes, as opposed to the previous example that was driven by sixteenth notes.

MODERN R&B

A great deal of the R&B played today features bass lines played on keyboards or sequenced through computers. The lines are also more likely to follow the bass drum more closely or exactly. Still, artists such as Meshell Ndegeocello, Erykah Badu, and D'Angelo make extensive use of bass guitar in their music as well. Look at this example of how a modern R&B bass line could sound.

- The use of octave notes isn't new to R&B music, but it has added emphasis due to the influence of the expanded reach of keyboards.
- Keyboards also have a lower range than most bass guitars, which is one reason behind the development of 5- and 6-string bass guitars.

Again, there's more to R&B music than could be explained here. Look to artists such as James Jamerson, Donald "Duck" Dunn, Bootsy Collins, Willie Weeks, and others to see where soul, funk, and R&B music were born.

Reggae was born from a combination of R&B and island and African rhythms. It's a sound naturally tied to the island of Jamaica, where it was born.

What Distinguishes Reggae Bass

DROP THE ONE

Whereas R&B puts the emphasis heavily on the first beat of the measure, reggae gets a characteristic feel from *not* playing on the first beat. Because the bass guitar plays a huge part of that rhythm, it's not uncommon to see parts like this:

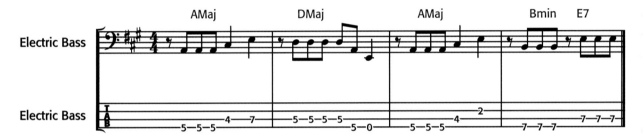

- Notice how each measure begins with an eighth-note rest.
- Many reggae parts are based around arpeggios. Notice how the part outlines each chord.
- Respect the space in this part. It defines the groove as much as the notes that are played.

LISTEN UP

To get a feel for how reggae should sound, listen to bassists such as Aston "Family Man" Barrett (with Bob Marley and the Wailers) and Robbie Shakespeare (legendary Jamaican studio bassist). Reggae is dependent on the bass, so listen well and maintain a bouncy, solid feel. This is another genre where you might want to roll down the high frequencies on your bass; reggae requires deep and rumbling bass.

FACT

Some famous reggae bassists
- Robbie Shakespeare
- Aston "Family Man" Barrett
- Flabba Holt
- Jah Wobble

Country

On the surface, country bass playing would seem to be the easiest style to play. The majority of traditional country bass lines feature only the root and fifth notes of each chord, and the notes closely follow the bass drum. There's a precision that goes with it, however, and the word "groove" applies here as much as it does to any other style of music.

What Distinguishes Country Bass

ROOT-FIFTH

The basic country bass line is shown in the following example:

- The notes are simple, and so is the beat. Just alternate the notes and give each one equal value.
- Notice how the root-fifth pattern is altered at the end of the third measure. This gives the line a little more motion, instead of staying locked on that one note as the chord changes.

This next example adds some rhythmic variation and introduces common country devices such as playing notes leading up or down to the root of the next chord.

- The sixteenth notes give a little push to the notes coming up in the part. They are eighth notes, and again this should be written out with each note given twice the duration that it has.
- The "walk ups" and "walk downs" to the root notes of each chord are common occurrences in country. Indeed, they're expected to be there to indicate when the chords change.

The last example is a valuable feel to master. It's also an easy feel to pick up because it's based on half notes. It's called the "two feel" because it includes only two notes per measure.

- There's a lot of space in this rhythm; however, be sure to give each note an equal value.
- This can also be played with quarter notes, adding quarter-note rests between the notes.
- You can also add little fills at the end of each measure, but keep it simple. Less is more in this case.

LISTEN UP

Everybody from the first Hank Williams to Willie Nelson helped define country music, so listening to that range of artists helps you get a better feel for country. For more modern country, the emphasis is as much on artists like the Eagles as Hank Williams, so incorporate that rock feel into your playing.

 TIP

Keep it simple, smarty!

The bass part often kept the tempo and rhythm for country music before drums were introduced to the genre. Keeping the part simple is the key to playing a country rhythm correctly. Playing only and exactly the right notes is often as difficult as playing many notes quickly.

chapter 11

Slapping and Popping

Slapping and popping on the bass guitar is a unique sound. No other instrument can produce this mix of tone and style, and it's an instantly recognizable part of any song in which it is used. Because it is so unique, however, it's important to find the right place and time for its use. This chapter helps you understand the basics and use it where it best fits.

Slapping Technique

The origins of slapping the bass lie with Larry Graham, bassist for Sly and the Family Stone. The technique was used to help replace the percussive sound of the drums on the bass guitar. There has always been a close relationship between the bass guitar part and the bass drum in popular music. Now you add the "thump" of that drum to the bass guitar's attack.

How to Slap

HIT THE STRING

With that in mind, it might be helpful to look at your thumb as the stick that hits the drum. Your goal is to hit the string with your thumb and allow it to bounce off, much like a drumstick. This gives you the percussive sound with the ring of the bass string afterwards. Refer to Chapter 3 for the basics of this technique. This chapter expands on those basics.

The power of the slapping motion comes from rotating the picking hand's wrist. The thumb itself is more of a striking object, and it doesn't actually move on its own. Use the body edge of the thumb near the knuckle to strike the string so that you get a clear, ringing tone after the first strike.

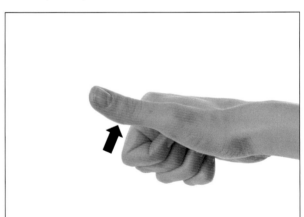

TIP

Let the string do some of the work

The string of the bass guitar looks like a spring, so it's easy to see how it can bounce back. Don't hit the string too hard, hoping to get the percussive sound. Hit it just hard enough to get the familiar slap tone, but let the string bounce back.

GET THE MOTION DOWN

The key of E is a popular one for bassists using the slapping technique because of the dramatic sound of the open *E* string being slapped. That makes this string a good place to start getting the slapping technique down. Do the following exercise:

1 Start by playing quarter notes on the *E* string using your thumb.

2 Repeat this exercise until you can consistently get a good, clear slapping tone.

3 Start with your metronome at 85 bpm and slowly work your way up to faster tempos. Move on only when you can hit all of the quarter notes on tempo with a good sound.

4 Practice these notes both *legato* (long and smooth) and *staccato* (short and choppy). To stop the notes while playing *staccato,* lightly rest your left hand on the strings to stop the vibrations. Then raise your hand just before playing the next note.

Now practice putting a rest on beats 2 and 4 of each measure, as in the exercise that follows.

Follow the same instructions for these measures as you did with the earlier examples.

Now play the notes in these measures on the *A* string.

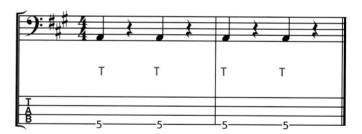

Play this example both on the open *A* string and the fifth fret on the *E* string. Raise your left hand off the fretboard to stop the note but don't let your hand actually leave the string. Then fret the next quarter note. Doing this helps you get your slap tone and technique down.

Popping Technique

To continue the drum metaphor, the "pop" of slapping and popping comes from the index finger pulling up either the *D* or *G* string to simulate a snare drum. A good way to approach slapping patterns is to think of a bass drum and a snare drum playing together.

How to Pop

PULL THE STRING

The pop comes from using the hook of your index finger to pull the string up and then let it slap back against the fretboard, producing both the note and a percussive attack. Again, this motion comes from the wrist, but it's produced by pulling up instead of twisting the wrist. After some practice, you'll find that the motion of slapping combined with popping comes naturally, and each action complements the other.

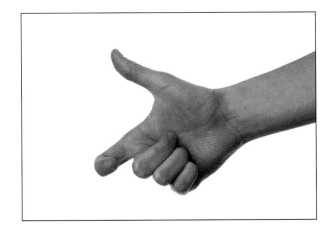

MAKE THE SOUND

Practice this simple exercise to develop your popping sound and get the feel of alternating thumb slaps and finger pops. T stands for a thumb slap, while P stands for a pop.

① Start by fretting the *A* on the *E* string, and fret the *A* on the *D* string, one octave up. This use of octave notes in slapping and popping is very common, so be prepared to see and hear it around a lot.

② Repeat this exercise until you get good, clear sounds out of both the slaps and the pops.

③ Again, start this exercise at around 85 bpm and move up the tempo consistently as you're able to manage both a good sound and correct tempo.

Now try putting the pop in a different part of the measure, as shown in the following exercise. The notes stay the same, but notice how the rhythm seems to change by placing the pops on different beats.

Practice these until you can consistently produce a good tone in time with your metronome. Getting these basics down will help you get ready for more complex patterns.

Remember also that most players choose to slap notes on the *E* or *A* string and pop on the *D* or *G* string. It's possible to slap notes on the *D* string as well; however, it gets difficult to produce a good note slapping on the *G* string because of the reduced mass of the bass guitar's thinnest string.

TIP

Listen to drummers

If you think of your thumb as a bass drum and the popped note as a snare, it makes sense to listen to drummers and see how they alternate those strikes. By hearing what these players do, you'll be able to expand the vocabulary of your own playing.

Some Basic Slap Patterns

The patterns in this section go a little further in showing you some different rhythmic and harmonic variations. Some of these are borrowed from funk, the breeding ground of slapping and popping; however, you'll notice that some of these examples could be moved to rock or jazz, where slap bass has also found a home. Feel free to experiment with tempos and keys as you play these examples.

Example Slap Patterns

BASIC SLAP PATTERN 1

This pattern keeps a steady quarter-note pulse, much like Larry Graham would play in his bass lines with Sly and the Family Stone. Use your thumb to play all of these notes. Because these notes are all played on the *E* and *A* strings, there's no popping of notes involved. The eighth notes at the end of the first three bars give the line a little more drive; the last few notes in the fourth measure give the example a *turnaround,* or a musical phrase that leads back to the beginning.

Play this and the following examples several times in a row until each time flows smoothly together. Start at a slow and steady tempo using your metronome. Then gradually increase the tempo, just as you did with the other examples.

BASIC SLAP PATTERN 2

This pattern adds a little more activity to the line, along with some popping with your thumb. The letters below the example show you how to play it. *T* stands for thumb, *P* stands for pop, and *HO* stands for hammer-on. That's fretting a note on a string with enough force to cause the note to play. It's usually done on a string that's already vibrating.

Note the line drawn above the notes involving a hammer-on. That line indicates a *slur,* which basically translates to a hammer-on on the bass guitar.

BASIC SLAP PATTERN 3

This slap pattern speeds up everything a little more by using sixteenth notes at the beginning, and it puts the riff into a minor key. Pay attention to the difference between the hammer-on at the beginning and the notes later in the first measure. The hammer-on should have a flowing feel, which contrasts well with the pronounced notes in the second part.

Also note the dotted eighth note at the beginning of the second measure. Remember that this means the note has one-and-a-half times the value of the normal eighth note. That gives the music a little lag, which makes it a little funkier than just playing it straight.

CONTINUED ON NEXT PAGE

Some Basic Slap Patterns (continued)

BASIC SLAP PATTERN 4

In this example, the rests have the dotted value, and the sixteenth notes should be played as a lead-in to the slapped octave notes. This pattern travels through a few chords, and it sounds almost like something that you would hear in the later work of the Red Hot Chili Peppers. Notice the last few notes in the last measure. Again, those are a sort of turnaround that indicate the pattern is *going back to the top,* or returning to the beginning of the pattern.

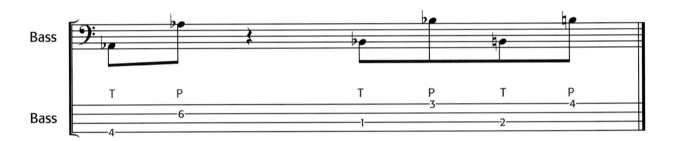

BASIC SLAP PATTERN 5

There are a lot of eighth notes in this pattern, but in reality you're just slapping the root and the octave notes and adding brief transitions at the end of the second and fourth measures.

Make sure each note has its own pronounced attack. They shouldn't blend into each other. A line like this would probably feel most at home in a disco-feeling song, although adding some distortion and compression to this sound could make the line sound good in a metal or industrial rock context.

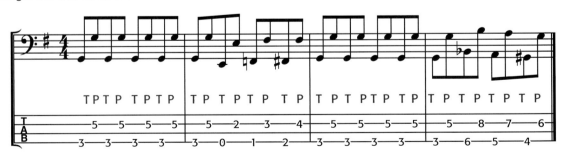

BASIC SLAP PATTERN 6

There's a lot of space in the line that follows. The beginning eighth note (or notes) at the start of the measures mark the beginning (known in funky circles as the "one").

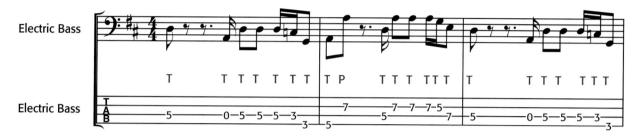

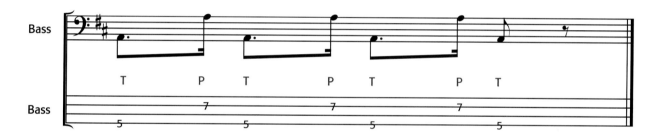

Sometimes, what you don't play is as important as what you play. These rests add to the line's sense of groove. Try playing it by putting a lot of emphasis on the beginning of each measure and playing the rest of the notes as lead-ins or transitions to the next measure. This line would work well in a funk or dance context.

BASIC SLAP PATTERN 7

The following pattern takes the disco pattern used earlier and adds some rests to break up the repetition. It also switches some of the emphasis away from straight thump-pop playing. This line would work well in dance or hip-hop music.

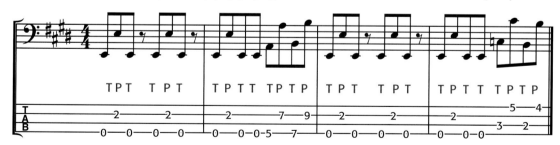

CONTINUED ON NEXT PAGE

Some Basic Slap Patterns (continued)

BASIC SLAP PATTERN 8

This last exercise wraps all of the concepts from this chapter into one example. Again, start slowly on this one until you can play each note with clear definition. When you can play this example several times in a row, speed up the tempo.

TIP

Keep the beat and the tune

It's easy to get caught up in the percussive nature of slapping and popping. All basslines still need a melodic and harmonic aspect to them as well, though, so don't lose sight of the notes you're playing. Make sure the notes get out along with the percussive effect.

MUTED SLAPS AND POPS

Remember also that slap and pop on the bass guitar is a very percussive attack, and sometimes muted notes or thumps can help drive a line along. Try slapping and popping the strings with your left hand muting the string (see Chapter 6 for more on muting), not fretting a note.

Play some of the examples again and choose notes to mute, producing just a percussive attack. These *ghost notes* drive the song along without producing a definite pitch, giving it a more percussive quality.

Slapping isn't appropriate for all styles of music, but it's a valuable addition to your playing style and quite useful on some occasions.

chapter **12**

Getting Your Tone

Just as important as what you play is how you play it. The bass guitar is capable of producing many different sounds, depending on what technique you use and how you adjust your tone and volume controls. This chapter gives you some idea of what directions you can take in your playing.

How Should You Play?

There's a long answer and a short answer to this question. The short answer is "Any way you want." As you learn and progress through these lessons, however, you're going to hear things you like and things you don't like. There will be styles you'll want to emulate, and there will be styles you won't care for. Ultimately, you're going to decide how you want to sound and how you want to play.

Types of Bass Playing

The longer answer is that each style has its own sound and conventions that define it. There's a reason why country bass sounds different than rock bass or R&B bass. The notes and rhythms play different roles in each of those genres. You should take the time to learn and study why players do what they do and sound like they sound. In other words, you should find out why it works and how you can do it. This doesn't mean you should only copy what other people do. Trust your judgment while you learn and find out what you want to do with your part.

Although they shouldn't be taken as hard-and-fast rules as to how you absolutely must play, the sections in this chapter will give you an idea of where to look to get your sound. From there, you should listen to the others you play with and help your style integrate with the song itself. You don't have to lose your ideas. You just have to support the music.

ROCK BASS

Although this category can include a huge variety of music, from lighter acoustic rock to AC/DC–style hard rock, there are a few common elements you'll find across the spectrum. In most cases, an even tone without too many highs or lows works well here. There's not a lot of distortion or overdrive here; however, louder rock might have a little additional grind to it. You might find some effects used here and there, but for the most part a simple, clean tone is a good choice.

Some common ingredients of a classic rock bass tone are a powerful tube amp, like the Ampeg SVT, and a heavy pick or plucking style. Listen to bands like AC/DC for a good example of tone and solid playing style.

CONTINUED ON NEXT PAGE

METAL BASS

First, start with the rock tone described earlier. Now, crank up the volume a little bit louder, and maybe crank up the distortion or overdrive pedal. Now, you have a metal sound.

Many guitarists in this genre have taken to adding lower strings to their guitars or tuning their instruments down anywhere from a half step to a whole step and more. That means the bassist often has to drop lower as well. Five- and six-string basses are commonly used, as are tuned-down four-string bass guitars. Both the lower frequencies (for a booming low end) and the higher frequencies (for a more grinding tone) are often boosted. Just be sure to keep the midrange frequencies present so that you can actually hear what the note is supposed to be.

The musical example here also shows a common technique – tuning the *E* string down to *D* for a lower, more sinister note. Notice in the tablature how the "0" on the *E* string stands for a *D* note now. You'll have to remember how the notes change when you tune this string down a whole step, but it can give you a little extra "edge" in your playing. On a five- or six-string bass, you would just play this note normally on the low *B* string.

JAZZ AND BLUES BASS

In the worlds of jazz and blues, the forerunner to the bass guitar was the upright bass. The classic jazz and blues sound strongly emphasizes the lower frequencies with a smooth, but not sparkling, high end. It provides the movement in the music without sonically getting in the way of the other instruments. The fretless bass guitar often is used in this genre to imitate the sound of its upright bass counterpart. This sound also works with Latin styles such as salsa and Afro-Cuban jazz. The following is an example of jazz bass.

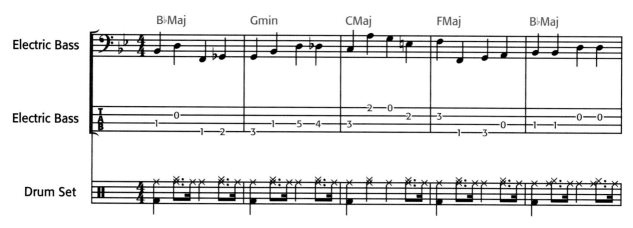

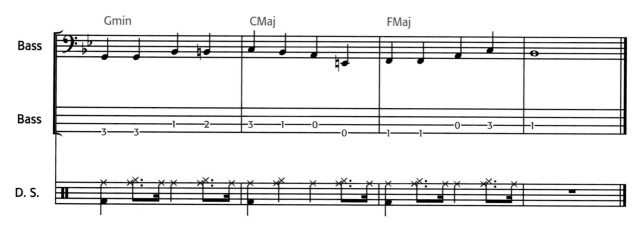

CONTINUED ON NEXT PAGE

Here is a blues bass example.

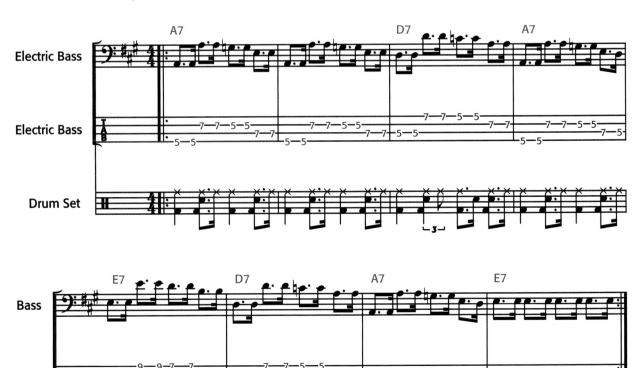

Especially with the influence of Jaco Pastorius, Marcus Miller, and other jazz bass guitarists, the bass guitar has also established itself as a potent lead voice in today's modern jazz sound. In this case, you hear a brighter sound with more emphasis on the high and mid-frequencies. Effects such as chorus pedals are often used here as well. Six-string basses are often used in this situation because they give improvising bassists more notes to choose from. Groundbreaking musicians such as Stanley Clarke even used the *piccolo bass*, a bass guitar tuned up a full octave. Use your best judgment as to what sound works best in any given situation.

R&B AND FUNK BASS

The bass guitar provides the bottom end in this style of music, both in terms of frequencies and in terms of making people dance. *R&B* stands for rhythm and blues, both of which the bass provides. A good R&B part will not only set a good rhythm, but emphasize the harmonies common to gospel and blues. The bass plays an important role here. It gets both the body and the soul moving.

CONTINUED ON NEXT PAGE

Funk takes syncopations and bluesy harmonies a step further, making it "nastier." Funk is all about dancing, and the bass makes people move. A strong low end is key here, especially since the advent of keyboard bass in pop and modern R&B. Some players use special effects, such as an octave divider, or actual bass synthesizer pedal, that actually reproduce lower notes and imitate the keyboard bass often heard in this music. You often see low *B* strings in this genre as well. Here is an example of a funk bass line.

Another standard accessory, especially in the world of funk, is the *envelope filter*. This effect gives the bass that slippery, almost vocal sound popularized by bassists such as Bootsy Collins in the 1970s. Picking up this pedal is a must for most funk situations, although a solid bass line is still the funkiest thing around. You'll read more about effects in Chapter 13.

Most instruments have a defined role in the band, and the bass guitar is no exception. The band counts on you to provide the rhythmic stability and basic harmony of the song; however, each player is looking for different things. This section addresses what the other band members are looking for.

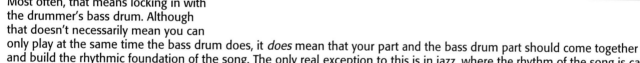

What Others in the Band Expect from the Bass Guitar

THE DRUMMER

The drummer and the bassist make up the nucleus of what's called the *rhythm section* of the band. It's obvious that the drummer's main concern is the rhythm and the "time feeling" of the song. The drummer is looking for you to sync up perfectly with his or her playing. That synchronicity is what provides the song's groove.

The drum set consists of several parts. In most cases, the drummer will keep a steady rhythm on either a hi-hat or ride cymbal. The snare and bass drums provide the skeleton of the song's groove, while additional drums (called toms) and cymbals (called crash or splash cymbals) are added for flair and musical embellishment.

Most often, that means locking in with the drummer's bass drum. Although that doesn't necessarily mean you can only play at the same time the bass drum does, it *does* mean that your part and the bass drum part should come together and build the rhythmic foundation of the song. The only real exception to this is in jazz, where the rhythm of the song is carried mainly on the ride cymbal. In this case, the bass is usually walking in quarter notes along with the quarter notes being played on the cymbal, thus creating the 'swinging' feeling that is the essence of jazz.

CONTINUED ON NEXT PAGE

Following is an example of drum set and bass guitar.

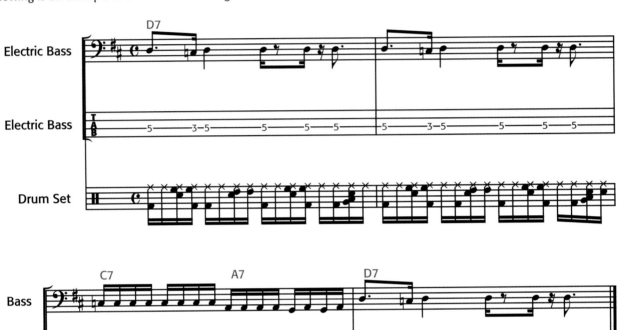

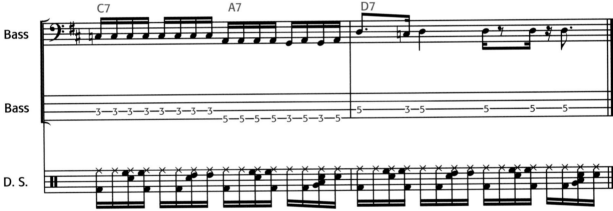

THE GUITARIST

Any rhythm guitar parts must fit in both rhythmically and harmonically with the bass part. Again, that doesn't mean a complete imitation of the parts, but it does mean that they must interlock. Sometimes, especially with rock or metal music, the bass and guitar play the same *riff,* or part, in unison. Other times, the parts are quite different. As long as they work together, it's a good part.

If the guitarist takes off for a solo, it's the bassist's job to keep the song moving and provide a good, solid bed for the guitarist's part. This might mean more room for a bassist to expand on his or her part, or it might mean the bassist has to stay home musically and play the part as solidly as possible. Depending on the style of the players in the group, you might need to play either role.

THE KEYBOARDIST

The keyboard is one of the few instruments capable of getting down into the same range of notes as the bass guitar, so both instruments need to take care that their parts are different enough to keep from making the low end a muddled mess. Other than that, the keyboards are similar in interaction to a rhythm guitar. They also function as a percussion instrument in a way, as they involve striking the keys while also producing a harmony part. The keyboard part should follow the rhythm of the drums and other rhythm section instruments.

Always listen to the other musicians in the rhythm section and try and come up with bass-parts that support everything else that's going on. These parts should provide enough rhythm or harmony for the song without being too overbearing. Think of the bass as a bridge between rhythm and harmony in the band, kind of like a melodic drum. Support and enhance the song, but don't get in the way of the other instruments.

VOCALISTS AND OTHER SOLOISTS

This category includes singers and other lead instruments, such as trumpets and saxophones. These instruments take their basic harmonic information from the notes you play, so they're looking for you to know all the parts of the song and define the song well. If the rhythm and harmony are taken care of, the soloists feel comfortable with their playing and can deliver a strong performance.

Dialing It In on Active and Passive Bass Guitars

The most basic tone controls for your playing lie in your fingers. The bass guitar has a different tone depending on how hard you play and what part of your hand you use to strike the note. Beyond that, you can use the electronics in your bass guitar to significantly alter the tone of your playing.

Passive Bass Guitars

There's nothing necessarily passive about bass guitars. In this case, the term *passive* refers to the nature of the electronics used in the pickups of the instrument. Because there are no preamps or power sources involved in the signal path of the bass guitar, the controls can only reduce or raise the volume or types of frequencies coming from the instrument.

The controls on passive bass guitars tend to be fairly simple. Generally, there are controls for volume (either one for each pickup or just one for the instrument) and a tone control. The tone control rolls off the high frequencies coming from the bass, emphasizing the lower end.

Still, it's possible to get a wide variety of sounds from the bass guitar even with these basic controls. By varying the amount of volume from the bass guitar pickups and changing the tone knob, you can get some classic sounds.

ONE PICKUP

If the bass guitar has only one pickup, like the popular Fender Precision bass (or "P-Bass"), it's a good idea to leave the volume knob up all the way while playing. The tone knob can be changed to go from a brighter tone to a more muted tone, although many players choose to leave that control fully up as well.

One pickup

TWO PICKUPS

For bass guitars with two pickups, such as the Jazz bass (or "J-Bass"), the tonal options are a little more varied. Each pickup has its own properties depending on its location on the bass guitar's body.

Pickups closer to the neck on the bass guitar tend to produce deeper notes that emphasize the lower frequencies. Pickups closer to the bridge of the bass guitar tend to produce notes that sound more focused and punchy, emphasizing the mid- and high-range frequencies. The tone control affects the full output of the bass guitar.

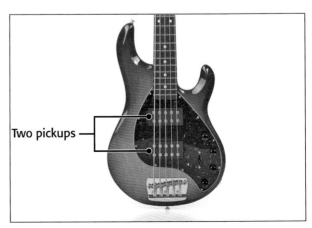

Two pickups

Customize Your Sound

You can customize your sound to fit whatever you're playing. If it's something that needs a great deal of definition from the bass notes, you can turn down the volume on the neck pickup to bring out more of the bridge pickup's sound and leave the tone knob up to its full level. If you want a more expansive sound that fills out more of the lower frequencies, turn down the bridge pickup and cut some of the tone as well. Playing closer to the bridge or the neck also emphasizes these sounds. The bridge will emphasize a tight, punchy sound; playing at the neck will create a wider, deeper tone.

Some bass guitars also feature a combination of the P-Bass pickup near the neck and the J-Bass pickup closer to the bridge. This allows the player to take advantage of both types of pickup tones.

It's a good idea to leave the tone controls alone at first and experiment with playing the strings in different locations on the body to hear what the natural sound of the instrument is before you start altering the electronics. The knobs will be there if you need to make more in-depth changes.

FAQ

What's that hum?

On Jazz-style pickups, turning down one pickup might introduce some unwanted noise into the signal. If this happens, try moving away from sources of interference such as neon signs, televisions, and computer monitors. Humbucking pickups, like those found on the Musicman bass guitars, usually avoid these problems.

CONTINUED ON NEXT PAGE

Active Bass Guitars

TONE CONTROLS

Active bass guitars have more tone-shaping options on board, thanks to additional electronics and power, usually in the form of small preamps and the nine-volt batteries that power them. These controls can boost frequencies as well as cut them. The additional power also makes these bass guitars louder overall than their passive counterparts.

The most common form of active controls offers high-, mid-, and low-frequency EQ controls. These controls take the place of the tone knob and allow more refined control of the tone. For example, boosting the mid-frequencies makes the bass guitar sound more pronounced in the mix, whereas many players cut the mids and boost high and low frequencies for use while slapping.

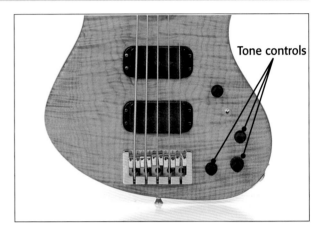

Tone controls

SOAPBAR PICKUPS

Active bass guitars usually feature the same types of pickups as the passive models. The main difference is the electronics behind these pickups. You'll also see larger pickups on these types of bass guitars, often called *soapbar* pickups for their blocky shape. These pickups can produce a wide variety of sounds, depending on how the manufacturer wired them.

SIGNAL ROUTING

Depending on the bass guitar, there might be several switches that change how the signal is routed through the pickups and electronics. There is a wide enough variety of these wiring options that they can't all be covered here. The basic physics are still the same, however. Pickups closer to the neck still produce deeper sounds, whereas pickups closer to the bridge produce more focused notes. Keep that in mind as you try out the various tonal options on the active bass guitar.

So Which Type of Bass Guitar Should I Pick?

There are benefits and drawbacks to each type of bass guitar. Although passive bass guitars might not be as loud overall as active bass guitars, the passive models don't rely on batteries to power them and don't run out of juice on stage.

Generally speaking, active basses are favored by players who want a more "modern" sound with a wide variety of tonal options. Those who want a more classic or vintage sound with a specific type of sound—and those who want a low-maintenance instrument—might gravitate toward the passive option. Ultimately, it comes down to what kind of sound is best for you. Try several different options and see which type is better for you and the music you play.

TIP

Different tools for different jobs

Most professional players own several bass guitars for different situations. One sound may work better for a show or recording than another. Your budget may not support this kind of collection, so start with an instrument that can be used in most situations and expand from there.

chapter 13

Buying a Bass Guitar and Amplifier

You walk into a large national chain or a small mom-and-pop music store, and you're immediately confronted with an overwhelming number of choices when buying a bass guitar and amplifier. Add the almost infinite possibilities of purchasing over the Internet, and you're looking at an avalanche of information. And all you wanted was a good bass guitar! This chapter tells you what to look for and how much you should probably expect to spend. You can get started for not a lot of money. This chapter will help.

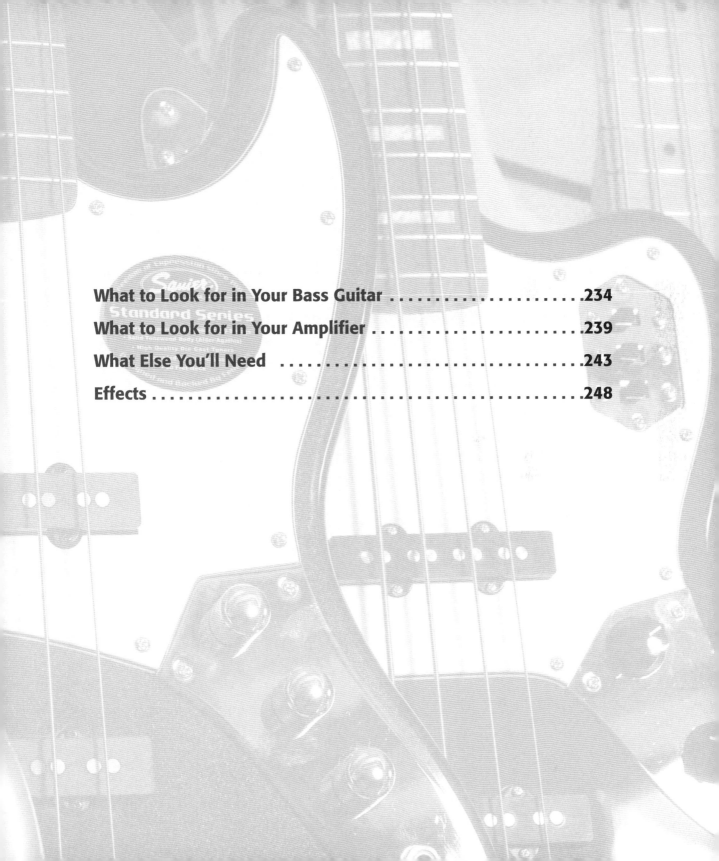

What to Look for in Your Bass Guitar

There is a huge variety of bass guitars available, in a large assortment of shapes, sizes, and configurations. Prices can range from just over a hundred to many thousands of dollars (plus time waiting for a builder to make your custom instrument).

The Bass-ics

At this point in your bass-playing experience, it's safe to assume that you can eliminate the custom boutique instruments that make up the high end of the cost spectrum. That shouldn't mean that you feel cheated out of quality in your instrument. In fact, you should expect the most out of your instrument, no matter what price you're willing to spend. There are some things that are not negotiable. Take a look at these now.

THE BODY

These are the aspects of the body you want to be concerned with:

- **The weight:** If your instrument is too heavy, you're not going to be able to focus on playing. Lift the bass and hang it on your body with the strap. If it feels uncomfortable, try another instrument.

- **The shape:** Play the bass guitar for a little while and take notice of the shape. Does it get in the way of your proper playing technique? Make sure the bass guitar both looks good and plays well before you buy it.

- **The finish:** The color of the bass guitar doesn't make a difference in how it sounds. It's okay to want a good-looking instrument, but remember that your first responsibility is to produce a good sound. Be sure to check for large dents or hunks of missing wood, however.

- **The hardware:** Make sure that the bridge, pickups, and strap buttons attached to the body are firmly in place. These parts can undergo a lot of strain, and it's important to make sure that they're solidly mounted.

- **The wood:** There are a few common woods used to make bass guitars, such as alder, mahogany, and swamp ash. Each of these woods have unique sonic characteristics, and each also differs in its weight.

Wood:	Weight:	Sound:
Alder	Light	Solid overall sound and resonance
Mahogany	Medium	Emphasized high end and woody timbre
Swamp Ash	Light	Emphasized midrange
Rosewood	Heavy	Darker tone, clear bottom end
Maple	Heavy	Bright and clear
Poplar	Light	Clean and crisp sound
Basswood	Light	Emphasized low end

CONTINUED ON NEXT PAGE

THE NECK

The neck of the bass guitar is placed under a great amount of stress by the pull of the strings staying in tune. Therefore, one of the most important things to check is whether the neck is straight. There should be a small amount of curve from the nut of the neck down to the neck joint. This is known as *relief*.

A simple way to measure whether there is a good amount of relief in the neck is to hold down an *F* on the first fret of the *E* string, and with the plucking hand, hold down the note at the 20th fret (or the last fret on the bass) and look down at the gap between the *E* string and the neck. The gap should be very small—maybe 2 millimeters. That will guarantee a playable *action* (the distance between the string and the fretboard). If the gap is any higher (i.e. 5 mm) the strings may be hard to hold down. If the strings lay flat against the neck, then the action may be too low and you may encounter fret buzz.

Keep in mind that the height of the strings above the neck can be changed by adjusting the bridge and truss rod. A trained professional should handle this. However, if there are excessive bends in the neck, these are more difficult to fix. Play up and down the neck in all positions and make sure there aren't any buzzes or quickly dying notes at any place on the neck.

More than likely, your first bass guitar is going to have a fretted neck. Check the frets on the neck to make sure that the frets are all glued down solidly and that there's no space between the frets and the fretboard.

These can create problems for you down the road, and you will have problems playing on them in the meantime.

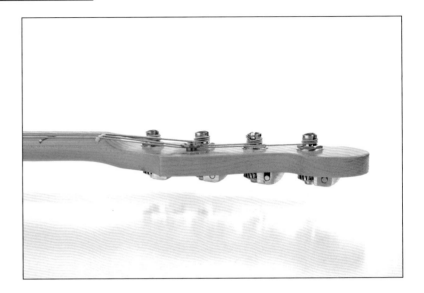

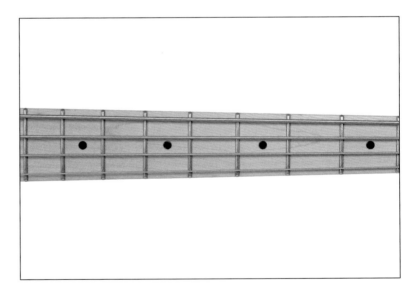

The nut on the neck should firmly hold the strings in place. The strings need to vibrate, but they shouldn't be allowed to slip from side to side or off the nut.

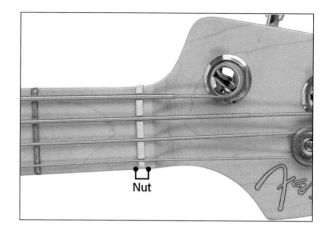

Nut

Make sure that the headstock is firmly mounted on the neck and that all of the hardware is firmly mounted on the headstock. The tuning machines should be firmly in place and should not allow any wiggling or movement. The tuning gears should also hold the strings in tune firmly without any slippage. If you notice the strings are constantly going out of tune, the tuning machines might need adjustment. The gears should also turn smoothly without any noise or grinding.

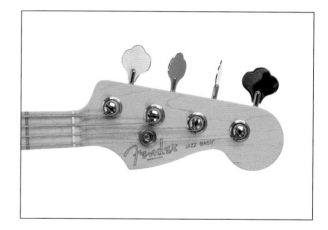

Finally, plug the bass guitar into an amplifier and play it for a few minutes. You shouldn't hear any scratches or shorts in the sound from normal playing. You should also be able to turn any knobs or flip any switches on the bass guitar without hearing any clicks, pops, hums, or scratches. If you do, it's probably a good idea to try another bass guitar, or at least ask the store to remedy the situation. It's also a good idea to make sure the output jack is mounted either in the body or on a metal pickguard. Jacks mounted to plastic are liable to break easily.

CONTINUED ON NEXT PAGE

THE COST

You can most likely purchase your new bass guitar for under $500. It's a good idea to buy the best bass guitar your budget will allow, but you can still get a good value at this level if all of the earlier-mentioned factors are right. More expensive bass guitars have additional features and better-quality materials; however, these aren't necessities when you first start playing.

BUYING USED

Like a used car, check any used bass guitar carefully to make sure everything is in shape. However, you can find some good deals on used instruments and still get a good sound. As long as the factors you looked at earlier are in place, you've got a good instrument. You might want to stay away from "vintage" instruments, which often command hefty prices for rare examples of certain types of bass guitars. Buying a used bass guitar that sounds good, however, makes a good deal of sense. There is also the added advantage that, if the instrument has been well looked after, it will have been 'played in', like breaking in a baseball glove.

TIP

Trust your ears, not your eyes

The looks of a bass guitar matter very little when you're playing the notes. Let how the bass guitar feels and sounds be your guide, as opposed to buying the shiniest or newest bass guitar. You want an instrument that performs well with you, not one you have to fight to play. Shop around and try several different types of bass guitars, taking your time with each one. You'll know when you find it.

The amplifier is an essential part of playing the bass guitar. After all, you've got to hear yourself to make sure you're in tune and playing the right notes. There are a few basic types of amplifiers, or *amps* for short, and you should know them in order to make the right decision.

Types of Amps

HEADPHONE AMPS

Like a portable audio player for your bass guitar, this type of amp allows you to hear your playing through a pair of headphones. It's a good option when you first start playing because it's relatively inexpensive, it allows you to practice easily, and it won't make a lot of noise to bother your neighbors. Even as you get better and move on to larger amps, this can still be a valuable practice tool for you because you can take it anywhere and play at any time. You can expect to pay around $50 to $100 for these.

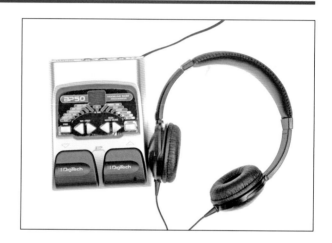

PRACTICE AMPS

Like headphone amps, these devices are used in practice situations. They usually have small speakers and limited power. They provide just enough volume to let you hear yourself, and they're also easily portable. These usually have anywhere from 10 to 100 watts of power. The cost is anywhere from $100 to $200.

CONTINUED ON NEXT PAGE

The Main Event

When you're ready to play live and be heard over a drummer, it's time to invest in a larger amplifier. There are a few things to take into consideration, however, so take a look at the various decisions you'll have to make.

TUBE AMPS

Believe it or not, old-fashioned vacuum tubes are still in use. In fact, many musicians insist on using them in their amps. Despite the fact that they can get very hot and are somewhat fragile, many swear that the tone these amps produce is second to none. They might not make good beginner amps because tube components are very heavy. Changing them also requires a professional or a lot of personal knowledge about electronics. Still, if you fall in love with the sound, nothing else will do.

SOLID-STATE AMPS

Solid-state amplifiers are made with modern transistors and electrical components, making them reliable and resistant to the crashes and drops that can sometimes happen to amps as they are moved or knocked over. They also require less maintenance than tube amplifiers, are lighter, and can be less expensive as well. There's also a wide variety of tonal options available, although some prefer what they hear as a warmer, more natural sound from tube amps. The best advice is to play both and see which one you prefer—and which one your budget allows.

HYBRIDS

Enterprising manufacturers have tried to combine the best of both worlds, putting tubes in the *preamp* section, or the section of the amp that shapes the sound itself. These amps use solid-state technology in the *power* section to amplify the sound, eliminating some of the weight and making the amp a little less fragile because there are fewer tubes to break.

COMBOS

Combos are called this because they include everything you need in an amplifier in one box. That includes at least one speaker and the amplifier. Just plug in the power and your bass guitar, and you're ready to go. There are several types of these available from different manufacturers in a wide variety of combinations, so you'll need to do some shopping to make sure you get what you need. Keep in mind these attributes as you go shopping.

- **Power:** To be heard in any sort of live situation, you'll need at least 200 watts of power behind you. As amps are turned up, they can sometimes overdrive the speakers and produce a distorted tone. Having enough power to be heard without that distortion is important.

- **Types of speakers:** Combo amps can include a wide variety of speakers and configurations. Smaller speakers (most commonly 10 inches wide) provide a great deal of definition and tone. Larger speakers (12 to 18 inches) give more bass tone.

- **Weight:** Because everything is in one box, they can be both bulky and heavy. You might want to consider buying one with casters or another transportation device if you don't like moving big, heavy objects.

HEADS

These devices include only the amplifier itself, without the speakers. This makes the unit lighter and more flexible because you can match it with different speakers for different sound possibilities.

These come in tube, solid-state, and hybrid configurations, like combo amps. They also come in power ratings from 200 to over 1,000 watts. The problem to keep in mind is what kind of speaker cabinets match your choice of amplifier. Ask the salesperson to make sure any speaker cabinet you buy has the same ohm rating as the head.

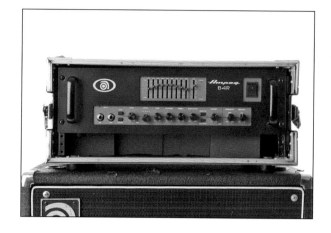

COMPONENT AUDIO

You can buy the preamp and power amp sections separately, mixing and matching to your taste. This is often the choice of professionals and audiophiles who know exactly what they want and are willing to spend the money necessary to get it. Until you get more experience and knowledge about these components, it's probably better to stick to combo amps or a head and speaker cabinet combination.

SPEAKER CABINETS

These boxes include from one to many speakers, depending on the configuration. Common types include two 10-inch speakers, four 10-inch speakers, or one 15-inch speaker. The more power you put into these speakers, the more cabinets (or higher ohm rating) you'll need. The ohm rating, or impedance, must match that of the head. Common cabinet impedances are 4 to 8 ohms. Again, ask the salesperson to make sure the speaker cabinets are compatible with the head you purchase.

CONTINUED ON NEXT PAGE

THE OVERVIEW

Now that you've gotten a look at the specifics of what goes into making an amplifier, there are some overriding concerns to keep in mind when you buy an amp to use in live performance.

Your power rating should be at least 200 watts if you want to be heard over a full band. If you're performing in a smaller venue with acoustic instruments, that can come down a little, but not much. It's a little unfair, but lower frequencies require more power to produce and be heard. That's why a 35-watt guitar amp seems as loud as your new rig. If you're playing extremely loud rock or metal, that power rating can go up to 500 or 600 watts.

Quality amplifiers vary in cost, but good factory-made combo amps usually range from $500 to $1,000. Mixing and matching heads and speaker cabinets can drive that cost closer to $1,200 or $1,300. That's why it's a good idea to start with a good practice amp, learn the basics, and then move up when you're ready to make an investment.

TIP

Make sure you can lift and move this equipment, either by yourself or with a small cart or casters. The amp isn't going to help you if you can't get it out of the store.

Now that you've got your bass guitar and your amp squared away, you're going to need a few other things to make your instrument sing.

Essential and Recommended Items

STRINGS

In addition to the roundwound and flatwound strings discussed in Chapter 2, there is a variety of materials and thicknesses to take into account. In most cases, strings are made out of stainless steel. Some are also nickel plated, and some are coated with special polymers to prevent corrosion. Some are even wrapped in black tape to dampen the sound of the string.

Thicker strings provide more mass, and therefore more volume and tone. They're a little bit harder to play than thinner strings, however. Thinner strings also allow you to bend and manipulate them more easily for more expression. Play different varieties and see what works best for you. Sets of strings range from $15 to $75, depending on manufacturer and materials. The "standard" gauges for a set of strings are .45 (*G* string), .65 (*D* string), .85 (*A* string), and .105 (*E* string).

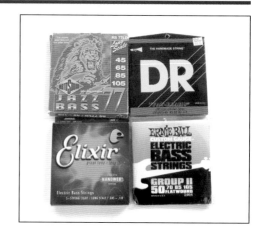

STRAP

The guitar strap allows you to play the bass guitar while standing up, and it can be helpful in playing while seated as well.

There's more to take into account than just the looks of the strap, however. There are several types of materials available, from leather to nylon to other man-made materials. Make sure that the strap you buy is adjustable, either through buckles or other methods, so that you can move it to the most comfortable length for playing.

A good guitar strap can also mitigate the weight of a heavy bass guitar as well. A wider strap with padding makes the bass guitar seat more comfortably on your shoulder, whereas a narrower strap might dig into your flesh and cause pain. Be sure that what you buy will be comfortable during hours of playing.

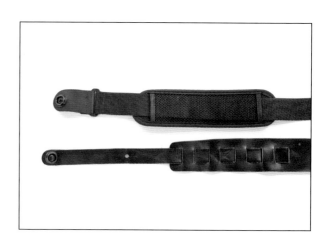

CONTINUED ON NEXT PAGE

There are also several different types of strap buttons, from the stock models that come with the bass guitar to special mechanisms that attach to the bass guitar and lock the strap in place. Make sure that whatever you buy is functional and keeps the strap in place without falling off. These mechanisms might also require drilling into the bass guitar, so keep that in mind when you buy.

CABLES

Cables connect the bass guitar to the amp, transmitting the signal that you'll eventually hear. There is a wide variety of cables available, all claiming to do some things better than others.

First, make sure the cable is long enough to allow you to move around without yanking on the instrument or the amp. Not only can this damage the cable, but it can also damage the jacks on the guitar and amp.

Make sure you can move the cable without crackling or losing the sound. Thicker cables better transmit sound from the guitar to the amp, and gold-plated connectors conduct electricity better than other metals, but this might not be of concern to the beginning bassist. As you progress, you might want to look into higher-end cables. For now, just make sure that they work.

After use, fold and properly store cables. To prevent damage, avoid bending them at extreme angles.

TIP

Velcro ties will help keep your cables in good condition. You find them at any hardware store and often at a music store. The cable should be wound in a circular fashion with no twists and then fastened with the Velcro to make a tidy loop. This is a good habit to get into from the beginning—untangling cables every time you want to play gets old quickly.

BASS GUITAR CASE

Your instrument needs a case for transport and storage. This is a nonnegotiable expense if you want to keep your instrument in good condition. Luckily, most manufacturers include a hard-shell case with your purchase. A hard-shell case is the best way to move your instrument. The hard plastic or wood takes the brunt of any shocks or drops you encounter.

A *gig bag* also protects your bass guitar, although not as much as a hard-shell case would. It is lighter and more maneuverable, however, and it often comes with convenient back straps. If you're carrying your instrument to a show, a gig bag will probably work. Make sure the gig bag has at least a small amount of protective padding. If you're throwing it in a van along with the PA gear, a hard-shell case might be better.

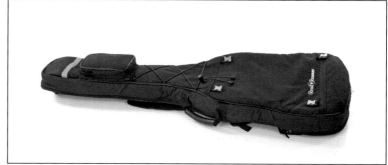

TIP

Traveling with your bass guitar

The bass guitar can react to extreme shifts in temperature, so be careful as you move your instrument around. Don't let it sit for long amounts of time in a hot car, and let it adjust slowly to moves from a cold temperature by leaving it in a slightly opened case or gig bag to warm up. It's a good idea to keep your bass guitar from sliding around a lot, so try to keep it out of the trunk and in the front or back seat of the car while traveling. Don't pile a large amount of gear on top of cases, and put bass guitars in gig bags on top of any pile. Finally, always carry your bass guitar in the cabin of the plane if you have to travel by air. It may take a lot of effort, but it's easier than arriving with a damaged bass from the potential changes in air pressure and temperature.

CONTINUED ON NEXT PAGE

GUITAR STAND

When you're not playing the bass guitar, it's important to make sure it's stored properly. If you don't keep it in the case, a guitar stand holds the bass guitar safely and prevents it from falling over. It's a must on the road and a good idea even at home. The average cost is $10 to $30.

TUNER

A good tuner is invaluable for making sure your instrument stays in tune. Expect to pay $20 to $40 for a good one. Make sure that it's made for bass guitar frequencies. Guitar tuners might not be able to handle the lower frequencies.

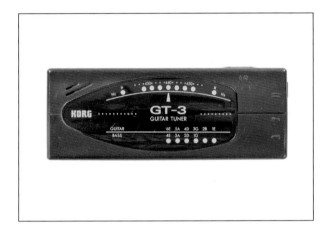

METRONOME

As discussed in Chapter 10, the metronome is a great tool in developing your rhythm. Make sure you get a digital metronome to keep a steady pace. Mechanical ones might lose some consistency toward higher speeds. More expensive metronomes might also include multiple beat patterns or tuning capabilities.

If you have a drum machine or computer around, you can also use these as metronomes using software or programs. You can even find free metronome websites on the Internet, so any computer can become a metronome with a few keystrokes. Just keep the beat simple so that you can focus on your rhythm.

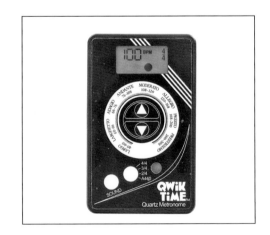

Toolkit

This is nothing as intricate as a mechanic's toolbox or woodworking supplies. These are just handy gadgets to keep around.

- **Soft cloth and polish.** It's a good idea to keep your strings and instrument clean. Use these to wipe down the bass after practice or performance.

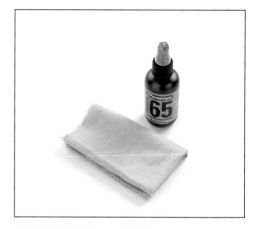

- **Wire clippers.** The process of changing strings is much easier with a pair of these around. Use them to keep excess lengths of string off of your headstock.

Note: Conventional wisdom regarding the amount of string to leave on the tuning pole is 'the more the better'. Leave enough so there are at least three or four full windings on the pole, but not so many that the string pops off the pole.

- **Screwdriver and Allen wrenches**. Your bass guitar probably came with adjustment tools. Keep them close in case of an emergency.

- **Extra strings, fuses, and tubes.** It's a good idea to keep a replacement item for anything that could conceivably fail. Better to have them around when you don't need them than to miss them when you do.

Effects

There's an entire industry designed around changing the sound of the bass guitar. You might not need all of the devices, but it's a good idea to know what they do in case the need arises.

Special Effects Devices

CHORUS

A *chorus pedal* essentially doubles the signal of the bass guitar, detuning it slightly to make the sound more full. This is a common effect for instances in which the bass guitar is performing a solo or filling out a great deal of sound.

COMPRESSOR

Another common effect for bass guitar is a *compressor.* This unit essentially evens out the sound of the bass guitar, making louder notes softer and softer notes louder. This makes the bass guitar tone more even, especially when you're using aggressive techniques such as slapping.

DISTORTION AND OVERDRIVE

Although both of these effects make the sound grittier and louder, they do so in different ways. *Distortion* modifies the frequencies of the signal, whereas *over-drive* simply cranks up the volume until it starts breaking up. Both are often used in solo passages and louder music.

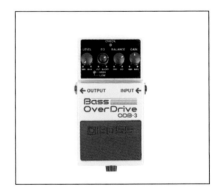

EQUALIZATION

Like your stereo or your amp, this pedal allows you to boost or cut frequencies. Use it to bring more (or less) bass out of your instrument or emphasize the high or mid-frequencies of your instrument. It's also often used in conjunction with other effects to round out the sound.

WAH PEDALS/ENVELOPE FILTERS

Often used in funk or psychedelic music, these effects give an almost vocal sound to the bass guitar. Think 1970s funk songs and movie soundtracks to get an impression of the sound. *Wah pedals* rock back and forth to modify the frequencies, whereas *envelope filters* modify the frequencies based on how hard you hit the strings.

Wah pedal

Envelope filter

Other Effects

People are always dreaming up new ways to make new sounds. From adding synthesized tones to making pitches go up and down based on a pedal, your imagination is the limit. Visit a music store to try out the pedals and see what's possible. Effects also come in multi-effect pedals (several effects in one) or rack units.

chapter 14

Care for Your Gear

Part of keeping your bass guitar and your amplifier sounding right is taking good care of your equipment. Although they aren't fragile pieces of china, you do need to practice some regular cleaning and maintenance to keep everything running correctly. From changing your strings to making sure you don't blow out your speaker, this chapter teaches you what you need to keep everything running correctly.

Before You Play

Even before you touch the instrument, there are a few steps you should take to make sure that your bass guitar performs well and stays clean and ready to go.

WASH YOUR HANDS

You don't have to handle your bass guitar with latex gloves and keep it in a sterile environment. However, your hands do have oils and dirt on them that can cause corrosion on the strings and make the finish on your instrument look dirty. Just a quick washing with a little soap makes a huge difference. Using warm water also helps you play by getting the blood flowing through your hands. So this one simple step helps both you and your bass guitar.

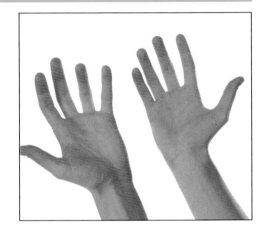

POLISH IT OFF

A little guitar polish brightens the bass guitar and makes it look good. If your bass has a lacquer finish, it's just a matter of putting some polish on a lint-free cloth and rubbing down the bass guitar until it's clean.

If you have a bass guitar with an oil finish, the manufacturer will tell you what kind of oil to rub into the guitar and how often to do it. The procedure isn't much different from finishing a piece of furniture. Be sure to follow the manufacturer's instructions, and your bass guitar should be ready to play for many years.

HANDLE WITH CARE

Accidents happen, and little nicks and scratches are inevitable. You can minimize these by following a few simple rules of care, however:

- Always keep your bass guitar in a case or on a stand when not in use. Accidental falls are a common cause of anything from chipped wood to actual breakage.

- Whether it's a belt buckle or that studded metal bracelet you have to wear during your band's set, keep your bass guitar from rubbing against any metal or other hard objects.

- Keep liquids and abrasive chemicals away from your instrument. This can damage both the wood and the electronics inside.

LET YOUR INSTRUMENT ADJUST

If you're moving your bass guitar from one extreme of temperature to another, such as from a hot car into a much cooler club or from winter cold to a warm stage, open your case and let the instrument sit there for a little bit before tuning or playing. Giving the bass guitar time to adjust before you put it under stress helps keep it intact. It's also a good idea never to leave your bass guitar in direct sunlight or in extreme temperature for very long.

FAQ

Do I need to buy a humidifier?

In a cold, dry environment, the wood in your guitar can dry out if you're not careful. If you plan to frequently store your bass out of its case, you should get a humidifier (a small, room-size humidifier will do). A humidifier will protect both the guitar's wood body and finish, preventing it from cracking.

After You Play

When you've finished playing, there are a few things you should do before putting up the bass guitar. Following these steps keeps your instrument looking good and sounding better.

Good Postplay Habits

WIPE OFF YOUR STRINGS

Your hands make the most contact with the strings, so that's where the most oil and dirt build up. It's important to get these materials off as soon as you're done playing because they cause strings to degrade sonically and wear out more quickly.

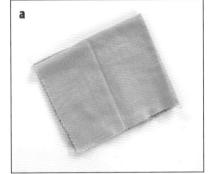

1 Take another lint-free cloth (a) not the same one you use to apply polish to the bass guitar body).

2 Wipe down the strings from nut to bridge when you're finished (b).

3 You can also use a small amount of denatured alcohol or commercially available string cleaners to take off particularly stubborn gunk.

WIPE DOWN THE BODY AND NECK

Yes, it's a good idea to clean the bass guitar's body and neck again after you're done. You don't have to do a full polishing; however, getting all of the dirt, oil, and grime off before you put the bass guitar back on the stand or in its case helps keep it in good condition.

LEAVE IT IN TUNE

It might seem logical that you'd want to loosen the strings to prevent additional wear on the neck and strings. However, the neck of the bass guitar is intended to hold the tension of standard tuning, so this is unnecessary. Furthermore, you're putting additional stress on the strings by constantly tightening and loosening them. Metal fatigue eventually breaks them, so go ahead and leave them in standard tuning.

PUT IT AWAY

Keeping your instrument on a stand (a) or in a case (b) helps prevent a lot of accidental damage. A falling instrument can escape with just a scratch or two, or it could cause significant damage to the neck, strings, or body, depending on where it lands. It's an easy step, and it'll keep your instrument ready to go.

You can use either a floor-mounted stand or a wall-mounted hook when the instrument is not in its case. Either works, but it's a good idea to keep a floor stand around in any case for use when you leave home with your instrument.

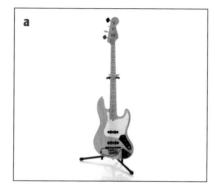

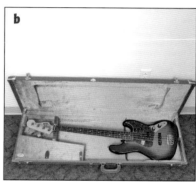

Change the Strings

There are two common reasons to change your strings. Either the strings have worn out from too much use and accumulation of grime, or they've broken. The former is up to you to decide, whereas the latter requires more immediate attention. In both cases, however, there are a few steps you can take to ensure longer string life and, more importantly, good tone.

Remove the Old Strings

You need the following:

- A set of new strings
- A set of wire cutters
- A tuner
- The correct screwdriver
- An Allen wrench

1 Cut the string just before the tuning machine on the headstock. Remove the string from the headstock and throw it away.

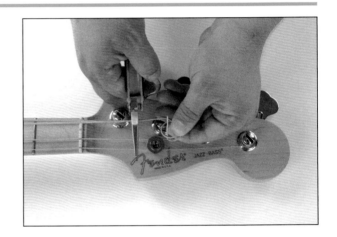

2 Pull out the rest of the string by the ball end.

Note: *Pulling out strings can cause the ends to flip around, possibly causing injury. Take it slow and pull out the string easily.*

3 Coil the leftover strings and throw them away.

Clean While the Strings Are Off

While the strings are off, you have a good chance to wipe down parts of the neck and body that aren't immediately accessible with the strings on. Follow these steps to get rid of excess dust and other accumulation.

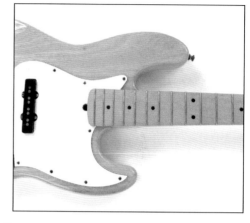

① Using a soft cloth, wipe down the head-stock and fingerboard, removing any dirt and dust you see (a).

② Using fingerboard oil or cleaner, apply a few drops to the cloth and wipe down. Wipe again without cleaner to remove excess (b).

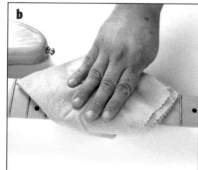

③ Wipe down the pickguard and pickups to remove dust and dirt. Use a Q-tip or similar tool to clean any areas between the body and the pickup.

④ Wipe down the bridge and saddles to remove dust and dirt. The saddles can be moved slightly, so go ahead and get under and around them.

CONTINUED ON NEXT PAGE

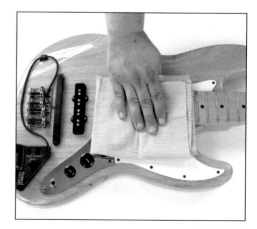

Now that the old strings are removed and the bass guitar is cleaned, you're ready to put on the new strings. Following these instructions helps you get the string on solidly without too many windings or going wildly out of tune.

Put on the New Strings

1 Remove the *A* string from the package and uncoil it.

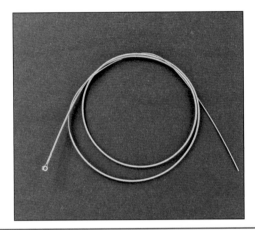

2 Thread the string through the bridge or body, depending on how your strings are held.

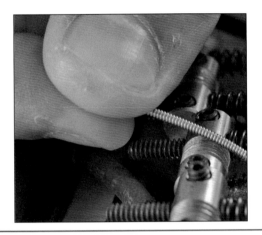

3 Turn the tuning machine for the *A* string until the slot is straight, allowing the string to lie flat with no bends. Put the string in the slot.

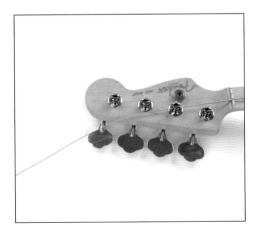

4 Bend the string around 2.5 inches to a 90-degree angle. Cut the string just after the bend, so that it looks like this. The bend helps keep the string from unraveling.

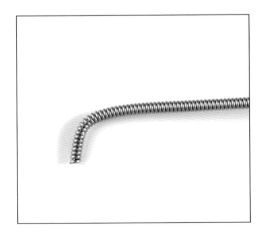

⑤ Stick the end of the string into the hole in the middle of the tuning machine. Bend the string at a 90-degree angle toward the bridge.

⑥ Holding the string in the tuning post, turn the tuning machine to tighten the string. The string should be pulled straight over the nut, without any angles. Make sure the string goes under any appropriate bars or string trees on the headstock.

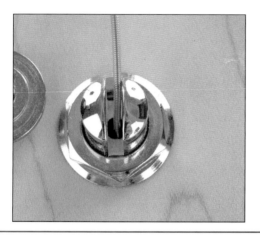

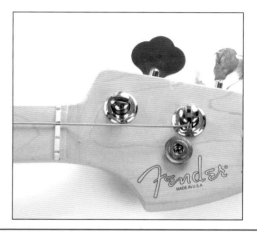

⑦ Turn the tuning machine several times to wrap the string around the post. Hold the string taut while you do this. Each wrap should go under the preceding one. This puts a little downward pressure on the string, making it easier to keep in tune.

⑧ Tighten the string until there are three wraps around the post.

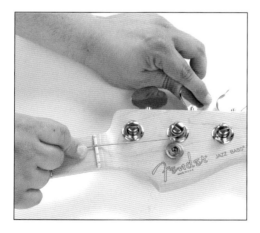

CONTINUED ON NEXT PAGE

⑨ Using the electronic tuner, tune the string to the correct pitch and then tighten it a little bit more. One or two turns of the tuning machine should work.

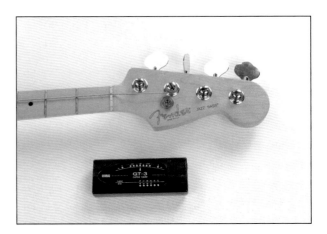

⑩ Tug gently on the string near the pickup. This helps loosen the string a bit, allowing it to hold its tune better in the future.

⑪ Tune the *A* string back down to pitch. You'll have to repeat this process at the end, but this keeps excess stress off the neck and the string for the time being.

⑫ Repeat this process for the other strings. It doesn't really matter in which order you put them on. You'll also notice yourself cutting less or more off the string, depending on where the string falls on the tuning machine.

⑬ When all the strings are on and stretched, tune up the bass using the electronic tuner.

Following these steps should keep your strings tuned and stable for however long you choose to keep them on. When they sound dead or stop holding their tune, it's probably time to change them.

A bass guitar's *intonation* is how in-tune the notes are across the fretboard. It's possible to have the open string in tune and fretted notes out of tune. A string's intonation is altered by moving the bridge saddle.

How to Check Intonation

1 Play the open string and make sure it's in tune.

2 Play the harmonic at the 12th fret (see photo) by lightly placing your finger above the fret and plucking the string. You should hear a bell-like chime. Using an electronic tuner, make sure the harmonic is in tune.

3 Fret the string at the 12th fret and play a note, making sure it's in tune using the electronic tuner.

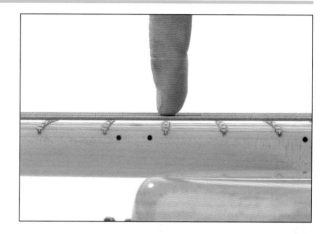

4 If the fretted note is flat, turn the screw at the bridge saddle to move it closer to the headstock. If it's sharp, turn the screw to move it away from the headstock.

5 Repeat tuning checks and turning as necessary to get everything intonated correctly.

If you're unable to get the bass guitar intonated or there are tuning problems at specific frets, have a professional luthier look at your instrument. It's possible that the neck or frets might need some repair work. This can vary from a cleaning and sanding of certain frets to a complete replacement of the fret wire. In any case, it's best to have the opinion and expertise of a professional to get your bass guitar sounding its very best.

String Height

String height, or *action*, is the distance between the strings and the fretboard. A lower action allows you to fret notes more easily; however, it also leaves you prone to producing more string rattle and noise. A higher action removes those concerns; however, it takes more effort to fret the notes cleanly and quickly. Trial and error will lead you to the correct setting.

Change Your Action

The fretboard usually has a slight curve, which the strings follow. This is called the *fingerboard radius.* Be sure to stay close to this curvature as you go.

1 Use the Allen wrench provided with your bass guitar or the appropriate substitute wrench in the bridge saddle. Make absolutely sure you have the right size, whether it's metric or English.

2 Turn the screws clockwise to lower the saddle. Turn the screws counterclockwise to raise it.

3 Fret the string at several places and play the note. If you get any buzzes or clanks, you might want to raise the string a little.

4 When you're happy with the settings, retune the bass guitar.

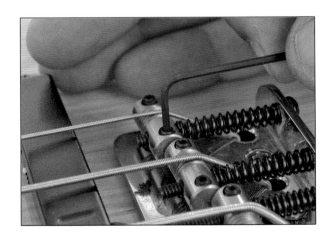

Again, if you notice any excessive clanking or buzzing on one specific fret or area of the fretboard, it might be time to bring in a professional. You might just need some adjustment to the truss rod, or you might have to have some work done on the neck or frets. In either case, it's best to have a professional look at it and make a determination about what should be done. The potential to cause serious damage to the bass guitar should outweigh any other concerns you might have.

Amps made today are usually fairly resilient; however, there are still a few simple steps you should take to prevent damage to the amp and/or the speaker.

Turn It On

It might seem obvious, but be sure you plug in the power (a) before trying to turn on anything. If the power switch is on when you plug in the amp, you might cause dangerous surges and speaker pops.

Likewise, if the amp has a speaker *off* switch (b), make sure you've plugged in and powered on the amp before you turn on the speaker. This again helps prevent speaker pops, which could damage or blow the speaker.

Make sure you've plugged your bass guitar cable into the amp (c) before turning it on. It might sound repetitive, but this could also produce a speaker pop.

If you're using any effects pedals that plug into a power source, keep them on the same circuit as the amp. If you plug into two separate power sources, you can introduce hum into the signal through a ground loop. Bringing along a spare power strip is a good idea in this case. Power strips with circuit breakers are even better.

Turn It Off

After practice or the show, follow these steps to keep your gear in working order for next time.

1. Turn off the speakers, if possible.
2. Turn off the power to the amp.
3. Unplug the bass guitar cable and coil it neatly for storage.
4. Unplug the power cable and the speaker cable and coil them, if possible.

With the speakers off before you power down and everything else taken down after the power is off, you stand less chance of harmful speaker pops.

Some Last Words

The earlier chapters in this book introduced you to the basics of the bass guitar. They also provided you with exercises and examples designed to improve your playing and your awareness of the bass guitar's role in a band. This chapter gives you some final words and concepts, and points you in some directions that you might want to go from here.

When you've mastered the exercises and concepts in this book, you'll have set a good foundation for playing the bass guitar. What you choose to do depends on a few factors.

Bass Guitar Resources

Especially with the advent of the Internet, there is a wealth of resources to learn from. You can learn something from just about any music, whether it's what you *do* or *don't* want to play. This section shows where you can get some more inspiration.

RECORDINGS

You've probably spent years listening to music as entertainment. Don't stop doing that just because you play an instrument now. But you can also treat what you listen to as tips and guides. By listening specifically to the bass lines in the music you enjoy, you learn more about how your new instrument fits into the overall scheme. When you listen, pay attention to these elements:

- When the bass guitar plays (and when it doesn't). Note how bass players gain more prominence in some musical styles as time progresses.

- The tone and sound the bass guitar produces. Notice how bass parts tend to become more pronounced and brighter-sounding as time goes on.

- How the bass guitar interacts with the other players. Study the relationships between the great rhythm sections.

- The history of the recording. Find out the circumstances behind the recording and how they led to the bass sounding like it did. You should also note the time the recording was made and the social and musical culture of the time, as this can give you a guide as to why the players chose to play the way they did.

LIVE PERFORMANCES

The added advantage of seeing performers is the visual cues you observe. You not only hear what the players sound like, but you also see how they play and can pick up additional information on their technique.

Don't get the impression that what you hear on the record is always what you're going to see live, however. Many performers choose to reinterpret or outright change their music in a live setting. Not only is this a good chance to hear something you've never heard before, but it can also give you some ideas on different playing styles and techniques.

Recordings can also be tricky propositions. It's possible to change and alter playing in the studio. When you attend a live performance, the playing that you see is real.

Choose from a wide variety of venues. Large stadiums or amphitheaters are usually host to the largest and most popular acts, but you might not get the best view of what the bassist and the rest of the band are doing. Smaller clubs and venues give you a better view, and you stand a better chance of actually picking up what's going on without the need for a large video screen or the earplugs that really loud concerts can require.

CONTINUED ON NEXT PAGE

MENTORS

Your mentors can take the form of either fellow musicians or a teacher or instructor. Seek out other bassists and pick their brains. A different perspective on your playing is often very valuable. By hearing how other bassists play, and letting them hear how you play, you can pick up advice and tips you might not have thought of before. The unique part about music is that although the notes may be the same, the interpretations are always different.

And don't be afraid to expand your scope to include other musicians in general. Sometimes, the most important lessons come from other musicians. You find out how they perceive their role in music (whether or not it revolves around them), and you take away something from it.

PUBLICATIONS

There's a wealth of information available on the bass guitar. You've got an excellent start with this book, but there are other sources you might want to consider.

- Magazines devoted to bassists and the bass guitar
- Books and anthologies featuring bassists and their work
- Sheet music and other written music

The important thing to remember is that there's always something more to learn. From here, you can look at different genres such as metal, funk, or jazz in much more detail. You can also read interviews and analyses of different bassists. Reading the words of these professionals can be quite inspirational.

THE INTERNET

Because the Internet is probably the world's largest repository of knowledge (both useful and otherwise), you can find a huge amount of knowledge and wisdom just searching around for your favorite bassists and styles.

Most famous bassists have personal websites for you to find out about their recordings and playing styles. You can also find many, many free sites that provide tablature or sheet music for your favorite songs. Bring up a search engine and let it run—there's no telling what you'll find.

Learn Songs by Ear

In the absence of written music (or the musician actually telling you how to play the song), you have to be able to learn the song by listening to a recording or other musicians playing. From there, you have to pick out your part in the song and play along. It might sound daunting right now, but following a few definite steps helps you figure everything out.

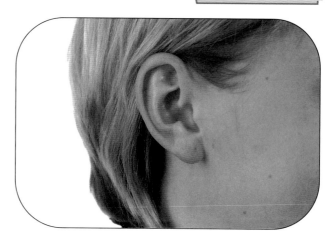

How to Play by Ear

LISTEN TO THE ENTIRE SONG

Break down the structure of the song. You should be able to find the verse, chorus, and bridges of each song. Listen to the song several times until you know exactly when each section begins and ends. Because most popular songs follow a specific and often familiar structure, you can learn the song more quickly by learning individual parts of it.

FIND THE KEY OF THE SONG

After you find out what key the song is in, you can figure out the chords and scales used in the song much more easily. Play notes on the bass until you find the one that sounds most at home with the rest of the song. That note is most likely the key of the song, so you should go from that discovery on to the next step of actually finding out what the correct notes and chords are throughout the song.

GET THE RHYTHM

Don't worry so much about the correct chords just yet. Right now, you want to make sure you can play along with the rhythm of the bass guitar part. Does it closely follow the bass drum, or does it instead follow along with the guitar part? Or does it forge its own way through the song, independent of the other instruments? When you've isolated the rhythm and where the notes occur, you can determine the pitch of those notes.

HIT THE RIGHT NOTES

Here's where you trust your ears and pick out the right pitches. Play along with the parts in the correct rhythms and you can hear the difference between the notes you play and the notes on the recording. Go back over these parts again and again until you get it right.

You can do this using a normal CD or digital music player, or you can purchase a specialized player (available at most large music stores and online) that allows you to slow down the song so that you can hear it at the correct pitch in slow motion. This gives you time to find the correct note before moving on. Before long, you'll have the part down and be playing along effortlessly.

Don't be afraid to make mistakes. Nobody will hear you do it, and they are only steps toward you being a better bassist.

Reading Music and Music Theory

There's an almost overwhelming amount of written music available to read and perform. The field of music theory is certainly large enough to warrant a lifetime of study. Luckily, however, you don't have to do this to play with your friends or a band. Picking up a little knowledge on reading music and theory can always help you become a better player, however. Don't be afraid to dig in and read up on the subject.

Sharpen Your Music-Reading Skills

You've already taken a big step toward learning to read music in this book. Most of the examples are laid out with standard notation and tablature to aid your learning process. Being able to read these examples is a valuable skill. But through repeated practice, you'll find it easier to read written music.

SIGHT READING

Sight reading is the ability to sit down to a piece of music you've never played before and play it with a minimal amount of prep time. This is a valuable skill to professional musicians, and it takes a great deal of time to develop. The process itself is easy enough to lay out, however. Just read and play through everything you can get your hands on.

Repeated practice of sight reading makes you more comfortable with the process, just like when you first started reading the written word. Through extended practice and repetition, you'll pick up the skill and be ready to go if the opportunity presents itself.

Just like a well-balanced diet, be sure to involve a wide variety of genres and songs in your sight-reading practice. It's a great way to break down the differences between these songs and genres and analyze both the notes and rhythms.

USE YOUR METRONOME

Be sure to include your metronome in these practices. You don't have to start at the correct tempo for the song. In fact, it's better to start slowly and build up the speed from there. You gain more control over the parts you play and develop confidence in your playing.

Work on Your Chords and Chord Progressions

By reading about and practicing different types of chords and chord progressions, you gain a better understanding of how they flow from one to the next in a logical manner. This may be of more interest to those who also write songs; however, the knowledge is valuable to those who are creating bass parts for other people's songs as well.

By looking at the common notes in each chord of a chord progression, you find what pitches work for a bass part that runs through the entire song. You also find the notes unique to each chord that give your part more depth and character. Knowing more about each chord helps you be a better player, even if you're playing only one note per measure.

Arranging

Arranging is the art of organizing the parts of many instruments so that they work together in the song. To do this, you must be able to understand not only the chords and the bass part of each song, but also the role of the other instruments in the song.

Again, this is a skill that most certainly benefits those who want to write their own music. But bass parts often change from playing a supportive role to doubling other instruments or playing a lead role before going back to a backing role. Learning what makes these switches possible helps you understand where you should play what part.

For example, a large and loud horn band isn't necessarily the place you want to try and take an extended solo. Your best bet at this point is to follow the roots of the chords and supply a solid foundation. Because there is so much activity happening in the other sections already, a busy bass part is likely to be lost in the shuffle. In a smaller ensemble, you have more room to explore and play a more active part.

Reading about arrangement techniques and researching the arrangements of famous groups and musicians shows you what's been done before and points your thoughts to new possibilities.

TIP

You'll see a great deal of arranging in the parts of big bands and jazz combos, as well as in television and film scoring. Read about these subjects to learn the secrets of those like Duke Ellington, Gil Evans, and Charles Mingus (a great bassist in his own right), who wove together elegant parts into masterworks of American music.

Appendix

Some Especially Noteworthy Bassists

One of the best ways to learn about the bass guitar is to listen to those who have played it before. The bass guitar is a relatively new instrument, but already several major players have established their musical identities and passed down their techniques to a new generation of bassists. This section introduces you to these players, gives you some information on their backgrounds, and recommends some songs that best illustrate their contributions to the bass guitar. Use this as a starting point to discover more music and add to your bass vocabulary.

Jack Bruce

Stanley Clarke

Les Claypool

Bootsy Collins

John Entwhistle

Flea

Larry Graham

Anthony Jackson

James Jamerson

John Paul Jones

Carol Kaye

Geddy Lee

Paul McCartney

Marcus Miller

Jaco Pastorius

Rocco Prestia

Chuck Rainey

Noel Redding

Chris Squire

Victor Wooten

JACK BRUCE

Playing in a trio gives a bassist plenty of room to find his own space and play expansive, searching bass lines. Having the fire lit under you by drummer Ginger Baker and guitarist Eric Clapton gives a bassist plenty of motivation to play bass parts that define how the instrument will be approached for years to come.

Jack Bruce simultaneously held down the bottom end for Cream and used his instrument to play long, intricate lines in jams that could last for over a half-hour. In addition, he wrote and sang a great deal of the material. After Cream broke up, Bruce released his own solo material and collaborated with many famous rock and jazz musicians.

Cream reunited in 2005 to play a series of concerts, and a new generation of musicians was reminded of the power and majesty of Bruce's talent. Even today, bassists would do well to listen to classic Cream recordings to hear what a gifted improvisational musician can do with the bass guitar.

Notable Tracks

- "Sunshine of Your Love," from *Disraeli Gears* (Polydor, 1967*)*
- "Badge," from *Story of Cream* (1983)
- "White Room," from *Wheels of Fire* (Polydor, 1968)
- "Spoonful," from *Fresh Cream* (1966, Polygram)

STANLEY CLARKE

Up through the Sixties, jazz and rock were distinctly different genres of music with little crossover between the two. As more and more musicians grew to appreciate both styles, however, it was inevitable that concepts would begin to blend. Thus was fusion born, and bassists accustomed to taking solos in jazz became more plentiful in rock.

Stanley Clarke is a notable doubler, or someone who plays both upright and electric bass. His work with Return to Forever and his solo albums put the bass guitar front and center. He often plays a piccolo bass, or a bass guitar tuned a full octave up, for solo work. He is also lauded for his slap bass and innovative compositions, which draw equally from rock, jazz, and funk.

You're more likely to hear Stanley Clarke in his film and television scoring work, although he continues to record and play live. He remains a vital influence on bassists everywhere.

Notable Tracks

- "School Days," from *School Days* (Sony, 1976)
- "Goodbye Pork Pie Hat," from *If This Bass Could Only Talk* (Sony, 1988)
- "Vulcan Princess," from *Stanley Clarke* (Sony, 1974)
- "Lopsy Lu," from *Stanley Clarke* (Sony, 1974)

LES CLAYPOOL

It's impossible to hear Les Claypool play bass guitar without immediately knowing who it is. His style is so unique and skewed that it could only be the work of the Primus frontman.

Claypool first burst onto the scene with his amazing combination of slapping, tapping, strumming, and fingerstyle playing in connection with the off-kilter rhythms of drummer Tim Alexander and guitarist Larry Lalonde. He eventually picked up a 6-string fretless bass and made even more whacked-out songs.

After Primus went on hiatus, Claypool played with Stewart Copeland and Trey Anastasio in Oysterhead, as well as his own solo project, Les Claypool's Fearless Flying Frog Brigade. Primus also recently reformed to play their classic material live, giving fans another chance to hear this unclassifiable talent for themselves.

Notable Tracks

- "John the Fisherman," from *Frizzle Fry* (Caroline, 1990)
- "Jerry Was a Race Car Driver," from *Sailing the Seas of Cheese* (Interscope, 1991)
- "Tommy the Cat," from *Sailing the Seas of Cheese* (Interscope, 1991)
- "My Name Is Mud," from *Pork Soda* (Interscope, 1993)

BOOTSY COLLINS

Most people think of a bassist as someone who stands in the back and plays solidly but quietly, with no flash. Bootsy Collins blew up that stereotype and quickly seized center stage with his funky playing and outlandish personality and appearance.

Collins was playing in a Cincinnati funk band when he came to the attention of James Brown. When Brown fired his band, Bootsy and his bandmates were on the next flight out to replace them. Collins worked with Brown to create some of the funkiest tracks of all time. Even so, Bootsy had not yet hit his peak. He went on to work with Parliament/Funkadelic figurehead George Clinton, who included him in his extended musical family. Collins also led his own solo effort, Bootsy's Rubber Band, with great success.

Collins continues to record and perform to this day, and his contribution to funk can't be measured. His use of fingerstyle and slap bass to "hit the one" has inspired a legion of funkateers to pick up the bass guitar.

Notable Tracks

- "Get Up, I Feel Like Being a Sex Machine," with James Brown (Polydor, 1970)
- "Munchies for Your Love," from *Aaaah . . . The Name is Bootsy, Baby!* (Warner Bros., 1977)
- "P-Funk (Wants to Get Funked Up)," from *Mothership Connection* (Polygram, 1976)

JOHN ENTWHISTLE

John Entwhistle found himself in a difficult place with his band, the Who. The band was already fronted by dynamic singer Roger Daltrey, provided with classic songs by guitarist Pete Townsend, and driven by hyperkinetic drummer Keith Moon. Entwhistle found his solution by turning up the volume and forging his own distinctive bass style.

Entwhistle played with a bright tone through loud amplifiers. He also used a distinctive right-hand playing technique. Instead of plucking the notes, he'd drum his fingers on the strings to produce loud, percussive notes that could stand up to the other forces of nature he played with.

Before his untimely death, he also played with many other rock legends and recorded several solo albums. Those efforts helped to cement his stature as one of the dominant figures in rock bass guitar.

Notable Tracks

- "My Generation," from *My Generation* (Brunswick Records, 1965)
- "Boris the Spider," from *Meaty, Beaty, Big and Bouncy* (Pye Studios, 1966)

FLEA

Raised around jazz musicians and equally at home in punk and funk music, Flea is one of the most recognizable bassists in today's popular music. His marriage of punk's energy and funk's sensuality helped propel the success of the Red Hot Chili Peppers.

Flea began his musical career aspiring to be a jazz musician. His friends drew him to punk and funk, however, and his work in the Red Hot Chili Peppers influenced a great number of rock bassists. His aggressive style of slapping can be seen in many music videos and has to be heard to be believed.

Flea has also worked with musicians ranging from Alanis Morissette to the Mars Volta, but his work with the Red Hot Chili Peppers will always be the standout achievement of his career.

Notable Tracks

- "Higher Ground," from *Mother's Milk* (Capitol, 1991)
- "Knock Me Down," from *Mother's Milk* (Capitol, 1991)
- "Fight Like a Brave," from *Uplift Mofo Party Plan* (Capitol, 1987)
- "Give It Away," from *Blood Sugar Sex Magik* (Warner Bros., 1991)

LARRY GRAHAM

Sly and the Family Stone were a groundbreaking group in many respects. Their music crossed the boundaries of rock and soul, and the band was a multicultural mix of race and gender. And bassist Larry Graham introduced a new technique to the instrument that blew the minds of many bassists after him.

Graham says that he began slapping and popping the strings of his bass to replace the loss of a drummer in an earlier group. In this group, it became a clear and present voice in the music. Graham drove the Family Stone's music with his distinctive playing style and slightly distorted tone.

Graham went on to lead his own group, Graham Central Station, and had a solo hit with "One in a Million." He's also collaborated with artists from Betty Davis (wife of Miles) to Prince. His legacy as a musician and innovator continues to resonate with fans of all genres of music.

Notable Tracks

"Thank You (Falettinme Be Mice Elf Agin)," from *Greatest Hits* (Sony, 1970)

"Everyday People," from *Stand* (Sony, 1969)

"Hair," from *Graham Central Station* (Warner Bros., 1973)

ANTHONY JACKSON

Taking his influence from rock and jazz bassists, Anthony Jackson went on to create a formidable career in both styles. Not only did he come up with one of the most recognizable bass lines in history for the O'Jays, but he helped to create a new form for the instrument itself.

Seeking to expand the reach of his instrument, Jackson helped design one of the first six-string bass guitars, or contrabass guitar. The additional high and low strings gave him much more room to improvise, and it was quickly adopted by many other players.

Jackson is an outspoken musician, both in his style of playing and his interviews regarding music. No matter what you think of his opinions, his influence on the bass guitar is undeniable.

Notable Tracks

- "For the Love of Money," by the O'Jays, *The Ultimate O'Jays* (Sony, 2001)
- "Feel Like Making Love," by Roberta Flack, *The Best Of Roberta Flack* (Rhino, 2006)
- "I.G.Y.," by Donald Fagen, *The Nightfly* (Warner Bros., 1982)

JAMES JAMERSON

Many bassists are easily identifiable by name or by group. You can tell exactly what recordings they appear on and where their band is playing on any given night. Yet one of the most influential bassists in history often went without credit on the records he played on, even as they climbed the charts.

James Jamerson was the house bassist for Motown Records, part of a group of musicians loosely referred to as the Funk Brothers. Motown was run like a factory, which meant songs were shot through an assembly-line process. Several teams of songwriters and producers would bring material to Jamerson, and the pressure would be on to produce a hit.

The Motown catalog stands as a testament to how successful Jamerson and the Funk Brothers were. Jamerson's lines propelled the songs and gave them an undeniable groove unmatched by anybody since. When you hear most of the Motown hits, you're hearing Jamerson. His musical voice was just as important on those recordings as anybody else's.

Notable Tracks

- "I Heard It Through the Grapevine," two versions, performed by both Gladys Knight and the Pips and Marvin Gaye respectively (both on Motown)
- "What's Going On," performed by Marvin Gaye, *What's Going On* (Motown, 1971)
- "I Was Made to Love Her," performed by Stevie Wonder, *I Was Made To Love Her* (Motown, 1992)

JOHN PAUL JONES

John Paul Jones was already an established session musician and arranger before joining the band that would make him famous. Following the dissolution of the Yardbirds, however, he would team up with Jimmy Page, Robert Plant, and John Bonham to form Led Zeppelin, a band that cast a long shadow over rock and heavy metal.

Jones was responsible for powering the group, along with Bonham's crushing drums. However, he also added keyboards and other instruments to Led Zeppelin, giving their bombast a more theatrical and intricate counterpoint.

Jones has remained busy as an in-demand sideman and solo artist; however, his legacy with one of the most influential rock groups of all time remains strong.

Notable Tracks

- "Achilles Last Stand," from *Presence* (Atlantic, 1974)
- "Black Dog," from *Led Zeppelin IV* (Atlantic, 1971)
- "The Crunge," from *Houses of the Holy* (Atlantic, 1973)

CAROL KAYE

Carol Kaye began her musical career on the guitar, but she left a far longer legacy on the bass guitar. One of the most recorded bassists of the Sixties, her work was instrumental in many of the pop and rock hits still revered today.

Kaye was a familiar sight in the studios of California, where she joined fellow bassist Joe Osborn, drummer Hal Blaine, and several others in the Wrecking Crew, a group of superb studio musicians. Retaining her pick from her days as a guitarist, she played the bass parts for artists ranging from Mel Torme to Glen Campbell to the Beach Boys. She also recorded hundreds of tracks for television, movies, and commercials.

Kaye is also noted for her teaching and writing on the bass guitar. Between that and her actual playing, Kaye personifies the rock-solid bassist who drives the song without getting in the way.

Notable Tracks

- "Good Vibrations," by the Beach Boys (1966)
- "Wichita Lineman," by Glen Campbell (Capitol, 1968)
- "Feeling Alright," by Joe Cocker, *Ultimate Collection* (Hip-O, 2004)

GEDDY LEE

Rush began its existence owing a heavy debt to Led Zeppelin; however, the band quickly evolved into a progressive force in rock music, pushing lyrical and instrumental boundaries into new and different realms. As bassist and vocalist, Geddy Lee is probably the most recognizable face in this band.

Lee's fingerstyle playing is both powerful and agile, neatly filling the space between highly technical drummer Neil Peart and abstract guitarist Alex Lifeson. Lee's monster tone and intricate lines set a new standard for playing in rock music.

Rush is one of the most long-lived rock groups in history, recording from the early 1970s through the present. Lee continues to be an inspiration on the bass guitar, even as he ably handles vocal and keyboard duties in the band's live performance.

Notable Tracks

- "Tom Sawyer," from *Moving Pictures* (Mercury, 1981)
- "Red Barchetta," from *Moving Pictures* (Mercury, 1981)
- "Freewill," from *Permanent Waves* (Mercury, 1980)
- "La Villa Strangiato," from *Hemispheres* (Mercury, 1978)

PAUL MCCARTNEY

As if being in one of the most influential rock bands of all time isn't enough to guarantee your legacy, there's also Paul McCartney's influence as a bass guitarist. Chances are that when you ask any bassist who inspired them to play, you'll hear McCartney's name.

McCartney not only held down the rhythm of the songs he played on, but he used the bass to add intriguing and twisting harmony lines to the songs. He was capable of playing simply, or he could orchestrate grand parts that gave a sense of majesty to the Beatles' songs.

Combine that talent with his songwriting ability and talent on other instruments, and you get an extremely influential musician. Still, whenever you see McCartney live these days, he's still laying down the bottom end with his bass guitar, just like he did on Ed Sullivan's show in the Sixties.

Notable Tracks

- "Something," from *Abbey Road* (Abbey Road Studios, 1969)
- "Come Together," from *Abbey Road* (Abbey Road Studios, 1969)
- "Day Tripper," single (Abbey Road Studios, 1965)

MARCUS MILLER

Marcus Miller is notable for his production work alone, and he's also a talented bass clarinetist. Yet his singular bass tone and amazing jazz and funk playing make him an idol of many.

Miller began his professional work as a studio musician, but he was quickly noticed and picked up by jazz artists such as Miles Davis and David Sanborn. His slapping style and bright tone are often copied. In addition to this work, he has produced and played for many other artists and singers, including Aretha Franklin, Luther Vandross, Bill Withers, and McCoy Tyner.

Miller continues to record and produce other artists, and he has a vibrant solo career. Miller's stature as a bass guitarist is hard to overestimate.

Notable Tracks

- "Tutu," by Miles Davis, *Tutu* (Warner Bros., 1986)
- "Teentown," from *The Sun Don't Lie* (Pra, 1993)
- "The Power of Love," by Luther Vandross (Sony, 1991)

JACO PASTORIUS

Although the bass guitar had become central to rock music by the time the Seventies rolled around, it had made a limited penetration into jazz. Monk Montgomery introduced it early on, and Miles Davis used electric bassists in his influential recordings. It took a genius, however, to simultaneously redefine the way a bass guitar would sound and break it into jazz music in a big way. It took Jaco Pastorius.

Pastorius began playing R&B and jazz in Florida; then he left his home state to tour extensively. Along the way, he developed a phenomenal technique that impressed musicians, record company executives, and fans alike. He played in the classic lineup of the seminal jazz fusion group Weather Report, and his solo album forced many bassists to reevaluate their playing. His fretless bass playing remains a standard for all jazz soloists, not just bassists.

Bassists owe an unimaginable debt to this player, who suffered an untimely death in 1987. Pastorius is a touchstone for all bassists in any genre of music.

Notable Tracks

- "Donna Lee," from *Jaco Pastorius* (Sony, 1976)
- "A Remark You Made," by Weather Report, *Heavy Weather* (Sony, 1977)
- "The Dry Cleaner from Des Moines," by Joni Mitchell, *Mingus* (Elektra, 1979)

ROCCO PRESTIA

Rocco Prestia is noted mainly for his work with the Oakland-based funk group Tower of Power, but his ability casts a far larger shadow over many other musicians. Prestia's fast fingerstyle playing gives an instant sonic signature to his group, and it makes him an influence for bassists around the world.

Prestia's sixteenth-note-based style blends seamlessly with the horn-based music of Tower of Power in a way that belies its complexity. That he can play such dense music that fits so well is a testament to his skill and ability as a musician.

Although recent health problems have forced him to cut back on his live playing, Prestia continues to pass on his style to new musicians seeking a different brand of funk and soul.

Notable Tracks

- "What Is Hip?," from *Tower of Power* (Warner Bros., 1973)
- "Squib Cakes," from *Back to Oakland* (Warner Bros., 1974)
- "You're Still a Young Man," from *Bump City* (Warner Bros., 1972)

CHUCK RAINEY

When you're a studio musician, the most important compliment you can receive is a phone call for more work. By that standard, Chuck Rainey is one of the most revered bassists in music.

Rainey's studio credits include work with everyone from Steely Dan to Aretha Franklin, and his partnership with drummer Bernard Purdie represents some of the highest points a rhythm section can reach. He's also worked on many soundtrack and television recordings, along with the big band of Quincy Jones.

Rainey remains a powerful force on the bass guitar to this day. The name might not be as familiar as some, but the tone and the style are instantly recognizable.

Notable Tracks

- "Peg," by Steely Dan, *Aja* (MCA, 1977)
- "What a Wonderful World," by Louis Armstrong, *What a Wonderful World* (Verve, 1968)
- "Until You Come Back to Me," by Aretha Franklin, *Aretha's Best* (Atlantic, 2001)

NOEL REDDING

Noel Redding started performing as a guitarist in Scotland, but a chance audition ended with him taking up the bass guitar behind one of the icons of rock and roll.

Redding played bass for the Jimi Hendrix Experience, meaning that he had to carry on the song with drummer Mitch Mitchell while Hendrix took off on one of his flights of incredible virtuosity. Redding could play basic riffs or outline the chords more melodically, depending on what was needed.

After Redding left the Experience, he played with a few other groups in America and his native Scotland. His most memorable work came from his collaborations with Hendrix, however. He passed away in 2003 at the age of 57.

Notable Tracks

- "Hey Joe," from *Are You Experienced?* (Experience Hendrix, 1967*)*
- "Fire," from *Are You Experienced?* (Experience Hendrix, 1967)
- "Manic Depression," from *Are You Experienced?* (Experience Hendrix, 1967)

CHRIS SQUIRE

Chris Squire stood out at a time when bassists were more used to a darker, rounder tone. In his work with progressive rock group Yes, Squire redefined the role of the bass guitar in a large rock ensemble.

Squire played a Rickenbacker 4001 bass guitar, which gave him a bright and springy tone that cut through the other instruments in Yes. His playing almost resembled a lead guitar part, so loud and aggressive was his playing. His style is instantly recognizable.

In addition to his longstanding work with Yes, Squire recorded his solo album *Fish Out of Water* in 1975. Squire remains an icon in rock bass guitar.

Notable Tracks

- "Long Distance Runaround," from *Fragile* (Atlantic, 1972)
- "Roundabout," from *Fragile* (Atlantic, 1972)
- "The Fish (Schindleria Praematurus)," from *Fragile* (Atlantic, 1972)

VICTOR WOOTEN

As a member of Bela Fleck and the Flecktones, Victor Wooten stood out as an amazing talent among an already stellar jazz fusion group. In his solo work, Wooten puts his more funky leanings forward. In any situation, Wooten is undeniably influential on today's bass guitarists.

Wooten is noted for his extremely quick thumb and fingerstyle playing, whether in his work with the Flecktones or his solo albums. Although his playing does involve an extreme amount of flash, he still brings substance to his songs. No matter what he does, his playing always enhances the song he's playing.

Wooten has recorded five solo albums, along with his work with the Flecktones and other jazz musicians. He also regularly teaches at his own bass and nature camp.

Notable Tracks

- "Sinister Minister," by Bela Fleck and the Flecktones (Warner Bros, 1990)
- "Me & My Bass Guitar," from *A Show of Hands* (Compass, 1996)
- "A Show of Hands," from *A Show of Hands* (Compass, 1996)

Index

Holt, Flabba, 201
Hood, David, 198
Howlin' Wolf, 154
humbucking pickups, 229
humidity, 253
hybrid amplifiers, 240

I

industrial rock, slapping, 212
interference prevention, 229
Internet resources, 268
intonation, 21, 261

J

Jackson, Anthony, 276–277
Jamerson, James, 198, 200, 277
James, Rick, 199
jazz bass tone, 221–222
jazz progressions, 162–163
J-Bass, 228
Jemmot, Jerry, 198
Jones, John Paul, 197, 277

K

Kaye, Carol, 278
key, 114
keyboardist, playing with, 227
key/time signatures, 102–103
knobs and switches, 14, 26–27, 230

L

lacquer finish, 16
Latin tone, 221
learning by ear, 268
ledger, 105
Lee, Geddy, 197, 278
left handed muting, 96
legato, 158, 207
leger, 105
lined necks versus unlined, 20
lines (music staff), 105
lingering style, 158, 207
listening for rhythms, 184
live performances, 267
low notes, tuning, 52

M

machines, tuning, 237, 254–255
major chords, 123–129
major scales, 126–129
major seventh chords, 135–136
Marley, Bob, 201
McCartney, Paul, 197, 278–279
measures, 105
mentors, 268
metal bass tone, 220
metal sound, slapping, 212
metronomes, 166–167, 246, 270
Miller, Marcus, 222, 279
minor scales, 130–134

minor seventh chords, 137–138
mnemonics for line names, 105
Montgomery, Monk, 279
Motown, 198
Muddy Waters, 154
Muscle Shoals, 198
musicians. **See** specific names
music notation. **See also** chords; notes; scales
    ACEG (staff space names), 105
    barlines, 105
    bars, 105
    bass clef, 102–103
    beats, 105
    chord names, symbols for, 147–149
    eighth notes, 104
    GBDFA (staff line names), 105
    half notes, 104
    key/time signatures, 102–103
    ledger, 105
    lines, 105
    measures, 105
    mnemonics, 105
    natural symbol, 103
    online resources, 112–113
    quarter notes, 104
    rests, 106
    scales, 114–118
    sight reading, 270
    sixteenth notes, 104
    staff, 105
    tablature, 111–113
    ties, 175
    triplets, 175
    whole notes, 104
muting the strings, 47, 95–99, 215

N

names of chords, 122
natural symbol, 103
Ndegeocello, Meshell, 200
neck
    buyer's guide, 236–237
    description, 18–19
    fingerboard, 19
    fretted versus fretless, 20
    illustration, 14
    lined versus unlined, 20
    overtightening the strings, 53
    truss rod, 18–19
Nelson, Willie, 203
notes. **See also** music notation
    above the 12th fret, 110
    dotted eighth, 174–176
    duration, 21
    eighth, 171–176, 194–195
    enharmonic equivalents, 107
    flat, 102, 114, 118
    frequencies, 107, 109
    on the fretboard, 107–110
    key, 114
    multiple names for, 107

Teach Yourself VISUALLY™ books...

Whether you want to knit, sew, or crochet...strum a guitar or play the piano...train a dog or create a scrapbook...make the most of Windows XP or touch up your Photoshop CS2 skills, Teach Yourself VISUALLY books get you into action instead of bogging you down in lengthy instructions. All Teach Yourself VISUALLY books are written by experts on the subject and feature:

• Hundreds of color photos or screenshots that demonstrate each step or skill

• Step-by-step instructions accompanying each photo

• FAQs that answer common questions and suggest solutions to common problems

• Information about each skill clearly presented on a two- or four-page spread so you can learn by seeing and doing

• A design that makes it easy to review a particular topic

Look for Teach Yourself VISUALLY books to help you learn a variety of skills—all with the proven visual learning approaches you enjoyed in this book.

0-7645-9641-1

Teach Yourself VISUALLY™ Crocheting

Picture yourself crocheting accessories, garments, and great home décor items. It's a relaxing hobby, and this is the relaxing way to learn! This Visual guide *shows* you the basics, beginning with the tools and materials needed and the basic stitches, then progresses through following patterns, creating motifs and fun shapes, and finishing details. A variety of patterns gets you started, and more advanced patterns get you hooked!

0-7645-9640-3

Teach Yourself VISUALLY™ Knitting

Get yourself some yarn and needles and get clicking! This Visual guide *shows* you the basics of knitting—photo by photo and stitch by stitch. You begin with the basic knit and purl patterns and advance to bobbles, knots, cables, openwork, and finishing techniques—knitting as you go. With fun, innovative patterns from top designer Sharon Turner, you'll be creating masterpieces in no time!

0-7645-9642-X

Teach Yourself VISUALLY™ Guitar

Pick up this book and a guitar and start strumming! *Teach Yourself VISUALLY Guitar* shows you the basics photo by photo and note by note. You begin with essential chords and techniques and progress through suspensions, bass runs, hammer-ons, and barre chords. As you learn to read chord charts, tablature, and lead sheets, you can play any number of songs, from rock to folk to country. The chord chart and scale appendices are ready references for use long after you master the basics.

designed for visual learners like you!

0-7645-7927-4

Teach Yourself VISUALLY™ Windows® XP, 2nd Edition

Clear step-by-step screenshots *show* you how to tackle more than 150 Windows XP tasks. Learn how to draw, fill, and edit shapes, set up and secure an Internet account, load images from a digital camera, copy tracks from music CDs, defragment your hard drive, and more.

0-7645-8840-0

Teach Yourself VISUALLY™ Photoshop® CS2

Clear step-by-step screenshots *show* you how to tackle more than 150 Photoshop CS2 tasks. Learn how to import images from digital cameras, repair damaged photos, browse and sort images in Bridge, change image size and resolution, paint and draw with color, create duotone images, apply layer and filter effects, and more.

Available wherever books are sold.

Visual®
An Imprint of ®WILEY
Now you know.